Maintaining Balance & Maximising Potential

By

Paul Wilson Bonner

Dedicated to
Sara
Bradley
Melissa
Mum

With Special Thanks to
Bill
Denise

Copyright © Paul Wilson Bonner 2011

ISBN 978-1-4709-7310-0

GURU-U

MAINTAINING BALANCE
&
MAXIMISING POTENTIAL

BY

PAUL WILSON BONNER

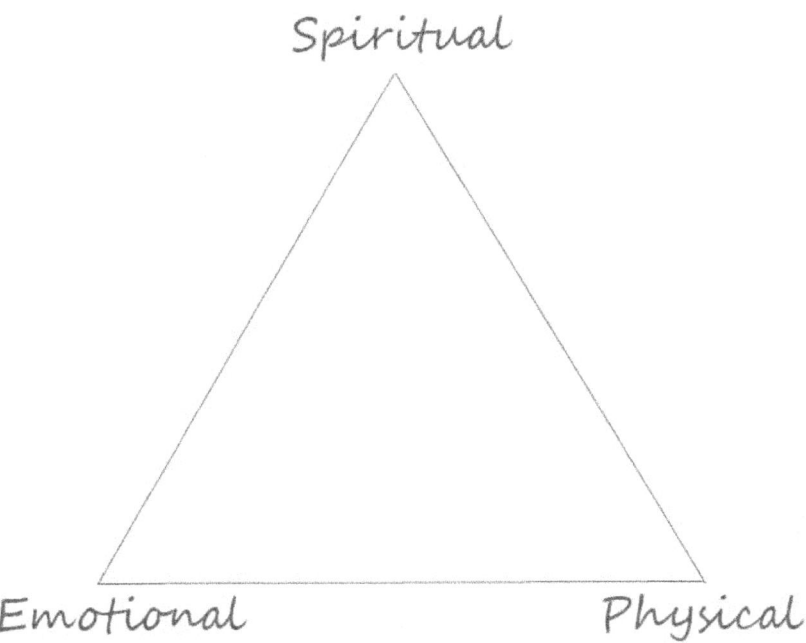

Three aspects

1. **Physical**
2. **Emotional**
3. **Spiritual**

1. Physical

1.1 Exercise
1.11 Choosing
1.12 Light
1.13 Walking
1.14 Moderate
1.15 Swimming
1.16 Yoga
1.17 Heavy
1.18 Gym
1.19 Aerobics
1.20 Martial Arts

1.2 Diet
1.21 Diet not Dieting
1.22 Bad Habits
1.23 Nutrition
1.24 Colloidal
1.25 Cooking
1.26 Variety
1.27 Choose your own weight
1.28 Macrobiotics

1.3 Prevention
1.31 The importance of exercise
1.32 Stress management
1.33 Acupuncture
1.34 Massage
1.35 Aromatherapy
1.36 Relaxation
1.37 Meditation
1.38 Chanting
1.39 Tai Chi and Qi Gong
1.40 Other examples

2. **Emotional**

2.1 Expression
2.11 Exploration
2.12 In touch, not out of touch
2.13 Negative/Positive
2.14 Anger/Rage
2.15 Nature/Nurture
2.16 Appropriate/Inappropriate
2.17 Time to talk
2.18 Men shouldn't cry?
2.19 The importance of good humour

2.2 Balance
2.21 Ego
2.22 Self
2.23 Others
2.24 Love
2.25 Money
2.26 Being still and quiet
2.27 Sex
2.28 Sleep
2.29 Time with family

2.3 Control
2.31 The illusion of control
2.32 Working in unison
2.33 Retrospective
2.34 Perseverance
2.35 Irritability/Annoyance
2.36 A few techniques

3. **Spiritual**

3.1 Wisdom
3.11 No matter what
3.12 A 'Higher Purpose'
3.13 You were meant to be happy
3.14 Turning poison into medicine
3.15 Self Empowerment

3.2 Faith
3.21 There is no Almighty
3.22 Finding a faith
3.23 Faith = Courage = Purpose
3.24 Not blind faith
3.25 Guru-You
3.26 Visualisation

3.3 Hope
3.31 Keep your eye on the prize
3.32 The difference between believing and knowing
3.33 Taking action
3.34 Trust in Guru-U

Learning

After a while you learn the subtle difference,
Between holding a hand and chaining a soul,
And you learn that love doesn't mean leaning,
And company doesn't mean security,
And you begin to learn that kisses aren't contracts,
And presents aren't promises.

And you begin to accept your defeats,
With your head up and your eyes open,
And with the grace of an adult, not the grief of a child,
And you learn to build your roads on today,
Because tomorrow's ground is too uncertain for your plans.

After a while you learn that even sunshine burns if you get too much.
So plant your own garden and decorate your own soul,
Instead of waiting for someone to bring you flowers.
And you will learn that you really can endure,
That you really are special.
And that you really do have worth.
So, live to learn and know yourself.
In doing so, you will learn to live.
(Anon)

Know Thyself

INTRODUCTION

Guru-U began to take shape as the result of a conversation with a friend. I told him "I'm thinking of committing my thoughts and ideas from the years I have spent in people development work to paper."

"Oh no! Not another self-help book? The world is filled with self-help books and courses and 'happy-clappy' workshops and conferences by self proclaimed modern day gurus. So why are *you* writing one?" he asked.

Good question. It made me think and seriously consider what I wanted to say without sounding clichéd. I realised that he was right. Most of the current works on this subject although wide and varied, seem to be 'just another self-help book' and to be missing the point. They skirt around the edges of the fundamental issues; how to develop and maintain a fully rounded and balanced life; how to really explore the causes deep within our lives that create the outcomes that we experience. Suggestions as to how to improve our lives are one thing, but practical solutions as to how to 'repair the damage' are something else entirely. It's like building a magnificent Cathedral without first laying the solid foundation, for no matter how fine the building, without a secure base, it will surely fall. We must first delve deep within our lives in order to expose the root cause(s) of our problems before we are ready to apply any effective and long lasting solutions. We must first prepare ourselves for improvement before we can actually improve.

"By writing this book, are you not just setting yourself up as yet another self-appointed Guru?" (My friend has a very cutting perception). He was right. What did I want to achieve by spending the long hard hours researching and writing?

Having spent many years as a martial arts instructor, youth development worker, a management training facilitator and as a life-coach I have been fortunate enough to be able to apply certain techniques to very real effect. I am, first and foremost, a human being, with my own mountains to climb and challenges to be overcome, and equally need to practice what I preach. I realised that not only was this precisely the way I lived my own life, but by offering this advice to those who seek it and seeing them applying the very same principles, their lives too have become more enriched and fuller somehow. In short, they have been able to *create balance* and *maximise their potential*, allowing them to deal with the stresses and strains of modern living.

The very essence of Guru-U is all about you the reader taking action and experiencing the benefits yourself. It is not about blind-faith or 'Guru worship', where you literally take somebody else's word above your own for the solutions to your challenges, as well as the causes, that lie within you and invariably with you alone. It is in a very real sense like having your own personal Guru who is always there for you, twenty four hours a day, seven days a week at hand to offer the best advice possible. The Guru within you that has experienced all that you have and consequently possesses the best insight into what makes you tick. What you like and dislike. What you are unable to do and what you have convinced yourself that you will never be able to do. This internal Guru knows far more about you than any external Guru ever will. It can propel you to take action towards creating outcomes that you never dreamed you were capable of. This may at first sound a bit fanciful and far-fetched, but as you progress and begin to suspend your disbelief and widen your horizons, it will become apparent and obvious and in time you will wonder why you have never done it before. Initially it's just a matter of trust. Trust in yourself and trust in your inner Guru, for you are the Guru, Guru-U.

I want to make it absolutely clear that by stating that we are all Gurus' to ourselves I do not wish to undermine the importance of guidance and support from others. For instance, if you want to become a doctor you simply cannot proclaim this to the world and begin practising as a doctor. You will need to spend years studying and learning from others in order to qualify even before you can begin to practice as a doctor. Every student must have had a relationship with a master and to have worked long and hard in order to acquire any skill.

However, when you have done so, as I have, you then carry the weight of knowledge and experience that makes you an authority in that particular field. I do not claim to be a master in all things but with those things that I have taken to time to learn and experience I do claim the right to comment. I certainly have no desire to proclaim myself as a modern day Guru as I believe that the solutions to your problems do not simply lie within the pages of Guru-U they lie within you. If you want to make a change in your life then first of all you have to want to change and then you and you alone, must take the action in order to see that change. Nobody else can do this for you.

"You must be the change you wish to see in the world."
Mohandas K. Gandhi.

Fortunately this does not require any specialist knowledge or years of training on your behalf in order for you to become an authority in your own life, just the burning desire to start moving your life in the direction of your own choosing. The fact is that you are ultimately the best qualified to judge for yourself, your own sense of balance and harmony within the world, your own sense of purpose and meaning and how well you think you are doing. No one is better qualified to observe your shortcomings than you are. It is you that have lived your own life and experienced what you have and taken each experience and moulded them into the person you are today, good or bad, rich or poor, it's all down to you. No one else can judge your experiences, for it will either be their opinion, which is just that, an opinion (and let's face it everyone has the right their own opinions) or it becomes merely an assumption, which to use the old saying to assume makes an **ass** out of **u** and **me**.

However, what I am not trying to do is offer yet another quick fix solution to the long term problems of living the rest of your life in complete balance and harmony with yourself and with the world. The solutions are proportional to the problems, so the longer you have been imbalanced the longer it will take to bring you back into equilibrium. This process, first and foremost, is a commitment to yourself and will require, at least in the early stages, for you to embark on a journey of self discovery in order to find out what it is you want out of life and how to go about achieving it. But, after a while, it will become second nature and you won't have to even think about it. It's a bit like learning to drive, at first was hard work where you had to use every ounce of concentration and after every lesson you felt so tired that you had to have a lie down. But after years of driving you get so used to it that at some time or other we have all experienced arriving home after a long journey and not remembering the last hour as the process of driving becomes that engraved on your subconscious.

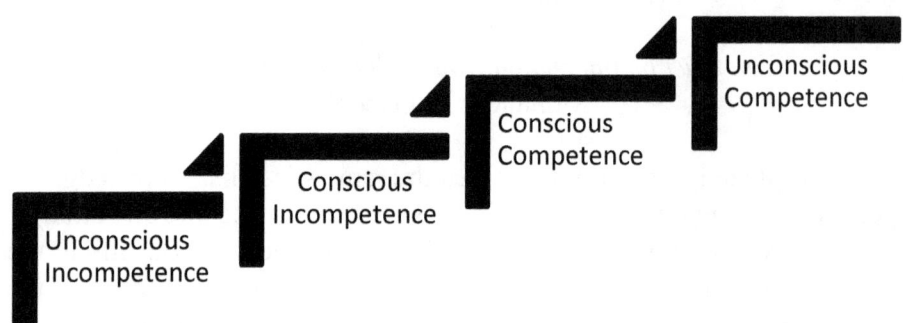

Figure 1: The Ladder of Learning

As an ex Martial Arts Instructor, Army Officer and as a professional Training Facilitator and Coach of many years standing, I have always enjoyed imparting the knowledge that I gained from actual experience, so that others could work on their own self empowerment. For example, I taught a group of women who, during the dark winter months, were virtual prisoners in their own homes because of their very real fear; the fear of not wanting to be outside during the hours of darkness. And let me tell you, during the winter Manchester, where I used to teach martial arts, is dark for a very long time. But by being able to teach them a few simple self-defence techniques they were able to transform themselves into strong and confident human beings that were no longer afraid and therefore released from their own chains of fear. Their fear wasn't replaced by bravado or foolhardiness but by genuine self-confidence that, should a situation arise they now had the confidence in their own abilities to look after themselves. Consequently their whole lives were transformed as they became more able to handle many other stressful and challenging situations, be it in their work, family or any other environment.

My motivation behind committing myself to writing Guru-U is simply to pass on some of the beneficial teachings that I have encountered for the benefit of others as I find that this has a profound impact on my own happiness. Seeing how each life becomes more enriched, mine too becomes more enriched. My desire is to impart these practical techniques far and wide for the creation of the self-empowerment for all those who wish to, once and for all, take control of their lives. For the benefit of not just themselves, but also for all their family, friends, work colleagues, and anyone and everyone else, they come into contact with. However, Guru-U is refreshingly different in that these techniques are not impractical teachings. No need to retreat to a monastery in the mountains. After all, to retreat means to move backwards. Self-empowerment means advancing! Guru-U is about applying practical solutions to the challenges and problems in everyday life, learned through actual experience and real life application.

We are all familiar with the term 'practice makes perfect'. When we practice it means that we must take action, which is often rigorous and sometimes painful. Like hard exercise, we feel a whole lot better afterwards (depending how out of shape we are in the first place). For some it will take a lot more work than others, but for everyone the results are the same, happiness, fulfilment and renewed hope for the future. Resulting in the courage to face life's challenges and setbacks with the total belief that we will not only overcome them but create a life of true value and purpose is the very essence of what Guru-U is aiming to achieve.

Science and psychology and some religions are finally catching up with the idea that the answer to all our problems lies within. That within us all exists an entity, our own personnel Guru, which can help us in dealing with all of the problems and challenges that each of us face in our everyday lives. It is capable of some remarkable achievements, like realising all our worldly ambitions for instance.

The good news is that you can take ultimate responsibility for your life and fully realise all of your dreams and ambitions. The bad news is it's you that also got yourself into the mess you're in right now! So long as you accept this basic premise and truly realise that action must be taken then I'm sure, like others, you will find these self-help principles both practical as well as extremely beneficial.

"To accept is easy; to continue is difficult." Nichiren Daishonin.

To begin to practice is always the hardest thing of all. It means that, first of all, you have to put yourself outside your comfort zone and into new and sometimes unfamiliar environments where you are forced to get to grips with the fundamental nature of your life (even, and especially, the not so pleasant aspects). Raising sometimes painful issues such as, "Am I lazy or am I driven?" "Am I happy with my life and do I want it to change?" Let me warn you here, if you are not ready to get to know yourself as you truly are then Guru-U is not for you, because sometimes the truth hurts. And at other times the truth we have been holding back from ourselves hurts like hell! As I said before, the good news is you are going to get exactly what you ask for, but the bad news is precisely the same! You're going to get exactly what you ask for! If you are fed up with poverty in your life and all you do is think about how poor you are, poverty will always materialise itself in your life. If you are continually challenged with relationship problems, you will inevitably suffer relationship problems.

This is because the mind knows no difference in thoughts, good or bad. They are what they are, impulses that guide us through our lives. But we as human beings have the unique capacity of turning our ideas into reality. For example, you need a job so you start scanning the adverts, sending out your resume and attending interviews and, lo and behold, you get a job. Okay you made all the effort, but in essence you predicted a possible future but more importantly you took the action to make it happen! So if you continually feel fed up, the more fed up you become. If you say to yourself "I'm tired" the more tired you'll feel. It's a kind of self-hypnosis. "You are feeling veery sleeepy. You want to go to sleeep." But more unerringly, if you feel unworthy, disliked, ugly, or stupid then the seeds you sow in your mind will reap that very harvest and therefore you will always feel unworthy and so on.

However, there is more to it than just having a Positive Mental Attitude (PMA). Because PMA says that if you continually say to yourself "I will succeed" or "I will make it" then you probably stand a better chance of doing so than if you take the counter argument, but only *probably*, and not always. The difference lies in augmenting PMA with something else. Something else that comes closer to guaranteeing your future well being and self-empowerment. And that is practice.

When I studied and taught a particular Martial Art called Ninjutsu throughout the 1980's, the one aspect I found most fascinating about this particular Martial Art was that it treated each person as an individual because, after all, we are all different in stature. Some are old, some are young. Some are fat, some are thin, some are men and some are women, and so on. Therefore as we are all different, how can two techniques be the same? What works for one person may not work for the next. As long as the end result is the same it doesn't matter what technique we practice.

I chose the word practice here very deliberately. Using the dictionary definition; to put in practice; to do or perform frequently or habitually; to exercise, as any profession; to commit; to teach by practice. So by definition we must commit ourselves to exercise (not just physically) frequently or habitually as if it were our profession! It's a sad fact that most people dedicate their whole lives to their career when in fact ones professional career is only around forty-five years, if you're lucky. But your body and peace of mind are with you for a whole lot longer. It makes a lot more sense to prioritise. Which is more important, your job or your life? That is not to dismiss the importance or ones career/vocation; it's all a matter of balance. But what I also like is that at the end of the definition, it says we that must teach others to do the same. How noble.

So we must all determine to make a plan of action which best suits us. For as the old saying goes "If you succeed to plan, you plan to succeed." Then, through a process of trial and error, we can establish a basic routine based on what we enjoy the most and are best at. Because, let's face it, nobody ever chooses to do what they are bad at. Then, and only then, will we be in a position to repeat the process over and over again until we perfect it. As any sportsperson or racer will tell you, that's the only way to win gold! But most importantly, this process must be as individual and unique as we are and I guess this is what separates the whole concept of Guru-U form others as they tend to be prescriptive, "follow the 10 steps" or "apply this tried and tested formula" to the point of saying "It's either my way, of the highway!" If you haven't succeeded then you missed out one of the essential steps. You either do it by the book or not at all. But I disagree as we all have different ways of going about achieving our own best possible outcomes, what might be right for some may not be right for everyone.

Here I wish to clarify the term 'Self-empowerment' which seems to be the latest buzz word, of which I am not the greatest fan, I wish to offer my own definition. The dictionary definition of empower is; *to give legal or moral power; to authorise.* Therefore we are authorised to give ourselves moral power, as if it were the law itself! And it is the only law that nobody, no matter how good or bad can escape from, the law of causality. It's pretty obvious really, if you do a lot of bad things, bad things are going to happen to you, and conversely, if you do a lot of good things, then a lot of good will come to you. But by 'moral power' I mean the power over our own lives and not to judge what is right and wrong for others and the power to commit ourselves to action, which is, when all is said and done, the overall and defining aspect of humanity. We think, we plan, we do, we become.

In short Guru-U is dedicated to all those who quest without compromise. To those who have read the books, been on the courses and found most of them to be of little relevance to their own lives and therefore less than helpful. But to move further means to go deeper into the fundamental aspects of our lives and like foundations, construct them in such a way as to guarantee our own individual happiness as well as those all around us. May the Guru within you lift you higher than you ever thought possible.

THE BASICS

Every martial artist will tell you that if you want to improve and make progress you must practice the basics every day. I once asked my Sensei (Japanese for teacher) Dr. Hatsumi, the 34th Ninjutsu Grandmaster, a very simple question; "How do I go from being a student to becoming a master?" With a wide grin he replied; "Practice the basics every day...for about thirty years!" Fortunately this practice is not as complex as Ninjutsu and should not take as long, depending on how balanced you currently are and how much work you need to do in order to align yourself to that place where you feel completely self-actualised, the place where you feel most fulfilled and truly alive.

At some time or other we have all (hopefully) had glimpses or periods when we feel this good about ourselves, who we are, where we are going and how we are going to get there. Everything looks certain and doubts are banished. But there are also other times when we feel out of kilter and certainly not performing our best. Self-doubt and negativity creep in. So what is the difference between the times when we are firing on all cylinders and cruising down the highway of life and those other times when we feel as though we have broken down at the side of the road as the traffic roars past us? Could it be that we are so busy living our lives that we sometimes forget and don't put enough time aside for ourselves? Could it also be that we have somehow forgotten, or even neglected, to do certain things that maintain our balance? I believe so for as in any martial art, the key is balance. A perfect martial arts manoeuvre is when we balance our speed, power and technique which produces the ideal martial artist, a master, or Guru if you like. This balance always forms a perfect triangle. No aspect is given greater or less credence than the other. The basic principle of Guru-U is that our lives too are based on the principles of triangular balance.

These three points are:

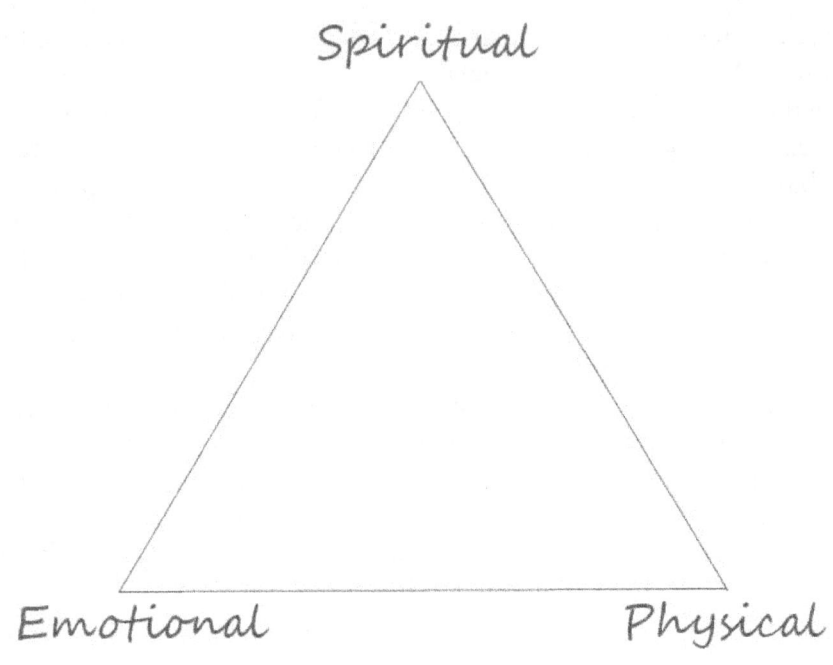

Figure 2 : Complete Balance

Our whole lives are built around these three simple principles. Many teachings concur with this principle and state that our balance is based on a perfect blend of our 'mind, body and soul', our 'health, wealth and happiness' etc. Consequently if each of these points is of equal importance and we are lacking in one area or putting too much emphasis in another then we are literally unbalanced. The sad fact is that the majority of people live their whole lives in a state of imbalance and never even know it. They concentrate their efforts, either out of ignorance or by choice, in one area and sadly ignore the others.

Imagine the mast of a ship. This is the central point of balance. Its ropes tightly lashed. Naval tacticians of years gone by knew that if you were to suddenly cut all of the ropes on one side of a ship it would lose its delicate balance and simply topple over. The same is true with our lives. The mast of our ship, that point of balance central to our lives is lashed with the ropes of us **physically, emotionally** and **spiritually**, none given a higher level of importance than the other, and if any of these ropes are not completely tight and in unison with the others then imbalance will inevitably appear in our lives which can lead to us metaphorically toppling over.

The basics of Guru-U are for you to look at these three areas, or fundamental aspects of your life, and work out which you are giving greater credence to and to examine those areas that you are currently neglecting. In order to maintain a perfect balance between your three fundamental aspects you must work on these areas of your life and therefore realise where you need to apply more or even less effort.

The simple facts are if you are too emotional or not emotional enough, this will inevitably create imbalance in your life. If you are too physical or not physical enough, then you will create imbalance in your life. And if you are too spiritual (a concept to be discussed in greater detail!) or not enough, then again, imbalance will inevitably show itself in your life. Therefore you have to lash the ropes of the three fundamental aspects of the physical, the emotional and the spiritual, to the mast of your life in complete and perfect equilibrium in order to maintain balance and to maximise your potential. To do this you must first understand each of these principles in detail and take the necessary action to bring yourself back into alignment.

Once you have achieved this is you will be back on the road of self-discovery and your journey to complete self-empowerment, self-realisation and self-actualisation will be back on track.

PART 1

PHYSICAL

Although all three aspects are of equal importance, to paraphrase the words of George Orwell *"Some things are more equal than others."* Without our physical abilities, complete balance is virtually impossible. Without a strong physical presence (and I don't mean the number of press-ups you can do) it is very difficult, if not impossible, to maintain ones emotional balance as well as expanding ones spiritual perspective. It is like planting a seed in sand or concrete, it just won't grow.

Most people are familiar with the theory of Maslow's Hierarchy of Needs where at the very bottom are our basic Biological & Physiological needs; such as air, water food, warmth and shelter. Way above those basic needs come our Belongingness and Love needs; such as relationships and affection, and right at the top are our Self-Actualisation needs; such as personal growth and fulfilment, which are covered in the later sections on Emotional balance and Spiritual balance. Therefore, coming from the standpoint that our physical needs are first and foremost we must investigate the best ways in order for us to build our physical aspect in order to build solid foundations.

Imagine trying to erect a building without the foundations from which to build. Without our physical facilities being in full working order how can we possibly contemplate any progress whatsoever towards Self-Actualisation and fulfilment? To put it even simpler, our physicality is everything. Our most basic physical functions are of course our heart beat, breathing, organ and brain function. Without these our emotional and spiritual aspects would simply not exist.

The old saying "If the flesh is weak, the mind is also" has validity for without the fundamental aspect of maintaining our physical centre then our health inevitably deteriorates. Without our health the Chinese triangle of Health, Wealth and Happiness simply come crashing down around us. There are many that are ill but rich and would gladly exchange their wealth for their health! After all happiness is not measured by ones bank balance.

Therefore we must first devise a plan as to how we can best maintain our physical aspect. This includes finding and maintaining a physical training programme, as well as looking at our diet and understanding how we can prevent illness and disease from happening in the first place. However, when I talk about physical training, what I am not saying is that everyone should become a professional athlete, far from it, as the techniques combined within Guru-U are wide and varied and take into account that not everyone is the same. There are always different strokes for different folks. So when our physical centre is balanced, greater stability occurs in all other areas of our lives. Once we have established a strong physical aspect our progress towards emotional and spiritual balance is inevitable.

The three areas that create physical balance are:

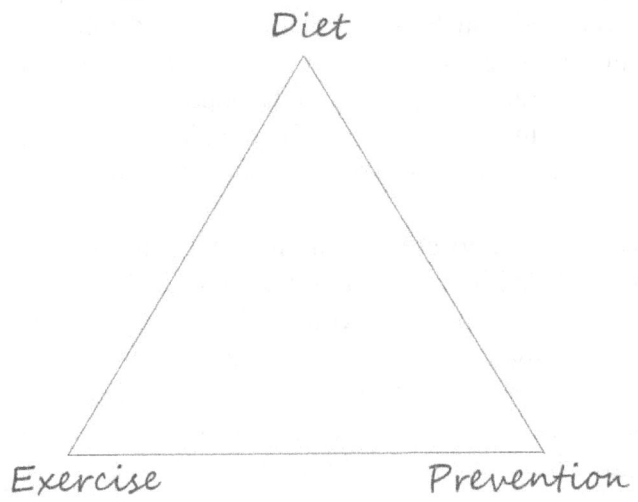

Figure 3 : Physical Balance

In the Exercise section Guru-U illustrates the importance of choosing an exercise programme that is ideally suited to you by considering the three main groups of exercise types; light, moderate and heavy as well as some simple activities for you to try e.g. walking, swimming, Yoga, working out at the local gym as well as other forms of exercise.

In the Diet section Guru-U will discuss topics such as diets not dieting, bad habits and nutrition, cooking as well as the importance of variety and choosing and maintaining your own weight.

In the section named Prevention rather than cure, Guru-U takes you through the basics of preventative medicine including understanding stress as well as some practical stress management techniques, the effectiveness of complimentary therapies such as acupuncture and aromatherapy as well as relaxation techniques including the importance of regular exercise in terms of stress management and illness prevention.

EXERCISE

1.11 Choosing

When it comes to choosing your exercise programme the first point to consider is the most important of all. It is **you** (or your Guru-U) that must decide what physical exercise is most suited to your own individual condition and no one else. Listen to your inner wisdom as it will guide you as towards what you most need to do. Please try not to allow others to dictate to you what they consider the best exercise programme because, let's face it, it's not them that is going to be doing the exercises for you now is it? I mean, friends and family may mean well, but what works for them may not be suitable for your own condition and/or needs. Also bear in mind someone else may find the prospect of you becoming fitter than them intimidating and will dampen your enthusiasm merely for their own self protection so be careful who you talk to. I'm not saying that you mustn't listen to their experiences at all, you should. You may well find that someone you know is getting great benefits from a particular exercise routine that you too could find beneficial. What I am saying is do not allow anyone else to *dictate* what you should or should not be doing, particularly if that influence comes entirely from the media.

The media is constantly bombarding us with the way we should look, what we should eat, wear and even think. All of our lives these false standards have been set, as if in law itself, by an industry where its prime motivations are simply for profit and the sad part is that the goalposts are constantly being moved. What is 'in' one season is 'out' the next. But one insidious constant seems to remain the same that fat is bad and thin is good.

But they have overlooked one important element. Your own Guru inside is impervious to the opinion of others. Your own Guru knows you better than anybody else and knows what is right or wrong for you. The media, and particularly the fashion industry, have been responsible for an immeasurable amount of suffering. You only have to see the totally image conscious concept of the elusive 'body beautiful' and look at the plethora of eating disorders that have resulted from this to realise that this is so. This has historically had more of a profound effect on women than men but today men are also being targeted to wear the 'six pack' stomach and emulate the pretty-boy models with tanned and oiled skins. No wonder most people feel unworthy. How can you possibly emulate those images of health and vitality?

As I said before, we are all different, but it is a sad fact that we feel as though we must emulate the look of others to feel accepted as part of society. How ridiculous. Society's unique qualities are based on variety, not on everything and everyone being the same. Look at our cities and the colourful tapestry of lives that make up our rich urban and suburban environments. Now imagine a place where everyone looked, dressed and spoke alike. Horrifying isn't it? And also ridiculous and totally impractical! So, what is the solution?

I believe that we, in conjunction with our internal Guru, should redefine our own boundaries as to what is right for us. It is up to each and every individual to tap the depths of their own innate wisdom to find their own image of health and vitality and not to be governed by the opinion of others. Some opinions are valid; some are not as they are merely opinions. Some bear the weight of factual evidence; others are merely based on whims and fads only to be proved at a later date as utter nonsense, or in some cases even dangerous and downright harmful. We all have the right to express ourselves as we see fit and what it takes for us to become fit and all we have to do is choose. Choose to either empower ourselves or allow our tastes and needs to be dictated by others. To begin that process all we have to do is choose an exercise programme that we like.

This gives us all the unique opportunity to choose for ourselves our own individual training programme. Let's face it, nobody ever chooses something they are bad at or will not enjoy. However most people still consider the prospect of sustaining any long-term exercise program with as much enthusiasm as visiting the dentist. Something we know that we have to do at some time or other but would rather put it off. But if you have a serious condition, like I used to suffer from, you cannot put it off forever. My own particular condition was that of a disc prolapsed in my back which resulted in years of agonising pain and discomfort eventually ending up under the surgeon's knife.

This is where you must change your thinking. So why don't you change your way of thinking and wake up to the fact that you already have a serious condition and you don't even know it yet? Yours is the condition of imbalance and should that undesirable condition remain then you are bound to pay the price for it at some time in the future when it may materialise itself as perhaps some form of physical ailment and/or emotional turmoil. The law of cause and effect states that if you do nothing about your situation then your situation will never change. But if you take action then things *will* change. So now is the time to act. Change your thinking and your perspective on exercise. Consider physical training in a different context. Try to consider it as a gift that you give to yourself, not a chore that needs to be completed. Imagine it as a treat that is equivalent to pampering yourself and taking a break at a health spa. Try not to consider it a task to be overcome but a pleasurable process to be performed. Professional athletes and dancers may look great but it takes a whole lot of hard work to look and feel that good and as any athlete or dancer will tell you, the pleasure is always worth the pain. But in your case the pain will be far less or more precisely, as much as you wish upon yourself.

So at last you finally have the chance to find something which you can really enjoy doing, so much so that you can maintain it forever, without that sounding like an awfully long time. I know that I look forward to the rest of my life with relish in that the activities that I have chosen to sustain my physical being are things that I look forward to doing. I find pleasure and a welcome solitude in swimming, cycling and walking my dog, and long may it continue. The most important thing here to bear in mind is, whatever exercise programme is going to suit you the best, it must stick to these three basic requirements;

1. **Light exercise.**
2. **Moderate exercise**
3. **Heavy exercise.**

A mixture of all three is essential in maintaining perfect physical balance. If one works too hard on one area and not enough in another then imbalance is the inevitable effect. But remember, this is your choice and the suggestions made are by no means an exhaustive list. If what I suggest does not suit your palate then choose from another menu, try to find something else that fits these basic requirements and most importantly can still be enjoyable.

It's also worth stating that if you are in what you would consider as 'bad shape' then you must only initially perform light exercise until you feel able enough to tackle moderate exercise. In some cases it is also worth taking the advice of your doctor if you have any medical history to consider. Listen to and trust in your Guru. It will tell you when the time is best. As babies we know when the time is to walk, no one else told us when to walk, we just did. When you want to run or swim or cycle or whatever it is also up to you.

1.12 Light exercise

Light exercise can include all kinds of activities that are designed to raise our pulse rates for periods of around 20-25 minutes. (Why that long? See cardiovascular charts in section 1.14 – Moderate exercise.) These could include very simple activities such walking the dog, cycling to the shops, housework or simply mowing the lawn. Thankfully this does not mean that we all have to rush off down to the designer gym and get our own personal instructor, excepting of course those who wish to do it that way. Light exercise can have a million and one different connotations but a single constant remains, we must move out of our comfort zone. This is the place where all our dreams of self-fulfilment are left dozing on the settee. We've got to get up and do something about it. All we have to do is use your imagination and add some spice to our lives.

I remember that in 1970 my mother must have been one of the first people to do what we now term as aerobics simply by putting on her favourite music (usually Abbey Road by The Beatles) and doing her exercise routine. I remember sitting on her feet while she did sit-ups, what great coaching for such a young lad. She would not just sit and watch television; she would work out to it! Lying flat on her back lifting her feet off the ground, hold for a minute, and then relax for a minute. However, even this may sound like extreme exercise to some. If it does, then why not consider just some simple stretching exercises?

You can do these either lying down or standing but whatever way you decide try to always follow this basic, work downwards from the top of your head to your feet. Start by moving your neck muscles, then your shoulders etc. These simple exercises are so easy that anyone can do them whatever your condition. They are a great foundation from which to build your physical centre. In some Japanese work forces they actually have a physical stretching session before each shift, why do you think that is? It's actually quite simple, when you engage your physical centre, you activate the others.

Bear this in mind. Although it may seem that you are just exercising your physical centre alone you must realise that your other two centres (emotional and spiritual) are also involved which have causes and effects upon each. For example your emotional centre is directly linked to your physical centre in that when your body is in good shape you tend to be less prone to stress. This is due to the powerful effect that your bodies 'natural high' chemicals such as endorphins have upon your neurological functions. Endorphins and serotonin are natural painkillers that are released during exercise and lead to a feeling of well being, even euphoria.

But on another level you must continuously engage your emotional centre when you exercise and light to moderate exercise is ideal for this purpose. Next time you take a walk for the purpose of light exercise try to also engage your emotional centre. How do you do this? It's simple. All you have to do is watch and listen! All you have to do is pay attention. As you walk past a tree or a bush don't just walk past it without noticing it. Ask yourself what colours are the leaves? Does it have an aroma? Observe the weather, the seasons, the details. You will find that 'mere' walking will become a pleasure to be savoured not a task to be completed and if you enjoy it then of course you will always want to do it again and again which is the key to finding an exercise programme that really works for you i.e. finding one you enjoy!

For example, when I swim I watch the shape of my hands underwater. Am I getting enough push on the water? I observe my body shape when I'm pushing off from the side at the beginning of each length. I notice the bubbles as I breathe out. After a while it becomes a subconscious act which then allows my mind to come up with some truly remarkable thoughts. Have you ever noticed that your mind always seems to give you the best suggestions when you are not really thinking about it? Some people say it's when they are in the shower or in the loo. For me it's when I swim. By thinking of nothing more than the movement of my body and the way I breathe it's as if my mind is able to rest. I imagine my Guru putting up his feet, reading the paper and having a cup of tea. Then he exclaims "Oh, by the way…" and the ideas come flowing.

Daily light exercise is crucial to keep all of 'our juices flowing'. My mother has now practiced yoga for nearly forty years and is remarkable for her age. She now does an hour every morning of what she simply calls her 'stretches'. She does not overcomplicate her own programme with all the names of all the postures. She has, through a long process of trail and error found a routine that suits her, and boy does she look and feel well for it! A regular exercise routine should become as much a part of our lives as a regular diet and regular bowel movements. Our bodies are like clocks that need to be wound up on regular intervals so that they will function efficiently. It is an interesting fact that the human foot has been proven to develop over evolution purely for the function of running, not walking. Although we can all walk on our feet and do so every day, the foot itself works at its optimum performance when running with all those tiny bones and muscles working in perfect unison. It has also been proven that those people who do not use their feet this way develop flat feet, fallen arches and the like.

Coming back to the reasons why some Japanese companies actively engage their workforce in physical exercises we must ask ourselves the reason why they do this. This is not something that they do for some obscure and undefined reason; in fact it has real bottom line implications. The workforce isn't asked to come in early so that they can do these exercises, this is actually part of their working day, and they actually get paid for it! So why take people off the shop floor, at some considerable expense, and not have them on the production line actually producing? The answer is quite simple, it pays them, in the long run, to have people functioning at a far more productive level for the rest of their shift rather than working at a reduced efficiency level for longer. It's far better to have people working at close to their optimum level of performance for shorter periods of time that it is to have people working at reduced levels of efficiency for longer. I have worked in various production companies where every process is given a ratio of time spent performing the task against actual returns, so why consume one of the most costly and valuable aspects of business (peoples' time) if it does not have a significant (not speculative or evidenced) return? When we engage our physical centre it kick starts the process of engaging our other centres. We can concentrate for longer, we can work for longer periods without the need for a break, we are actually more efficient and therefore a whole lot more productive, and that's the bottom line, by working smarter not harder, we significantly impact the bottom line. i.e. we make more profitable use of our time!

1.13 Walking

Walking is probably one of the best forms of light to moderate exercise as it can exercise the whole of the body, mind and spirit if done correctly. You're probably thinking 'What does he mean, if done correctly? I've been doing this stuff for years. No one needs to tell me how to walk'. Well that's just what I thought until I was inspired by the story of a man called Jock Lewes. Jock was the man who masterminded the whole training syllabus for the formation of the first Special Forces unit, the legendary SAS (Special Air Services) and truly mastered the art of walking. This may sound inconceivable but allow me to explain.

In 1941 in North Africa nobody knew how far we could walk in the desert and how much water we would have to carry. Nowadays all this information is readily at hand. We can quite easily look it up on some table or chart and by using the variables of temperature, humidity and the like calculate exactly how much water per hour we would perspire and need to consume. But in 1941 no one knew this and for the SAS's plans to succeed someone had to find out. Jock Lewes was that man.

He would choose a distance of around a hundred miles and carry a set amount of weight and water. He would then complete the journey (usually over a period of three days), rest up for a few days and try once more, this time with less water and more weight. Gradually he found the point where the human body could take no more. He would push himself to the very point of human performance to find the optimum limit. Once he found this limit he would then subject the rest of the men to this process. These challenges soon became SAS folklore and later where known as 'Lewes Marches'. Now, I'm not suggesting for a moment that we should all head out into the desert and walk for a hundred miles, far from it. What I'm saying is that we must use inspiration wherever we see it.

For me, I consequently developed a walking exercise programme when I was able to speed-walk for exactly one hour, do an about-turn, walk back from where I had come from and exactly on the mark of the next hour I would be within ten to twenty feet away from where I started. This is the way that we can build walking from light to moderate exercise.

First of all just pick your own time and route and most importantly time yourself. Get used to the habit of timing yourself and making a note of the results. Over the weeks and months you will be able to look back on these early efforts and realise how far you have come, literally and metaphorically. After a while you will certainly get to the point when your times will remain very similar, all you must then do is increase the distance. Just try five or ten minutes at first, whatever suits you best, and then increase the times by increments of five minutes at a time. Try at least two to three weeks with each timing then you can either increase it by another five minutes or leave it where it is. Remember that walking is the cornerstone from which to build. It's not meant to turn us into marathon walkers where all we do is walk. Let your mantra be 'everything in moderation', but not your excuse for not pushing yourself to higher limits.

Walking, when used as your sole exercise program will unfortunately create some imbalance, particularly with our intellectual centre, as walking does not require full cognitive function to be performed. Let me give you an example. When I used to teach Martial Arts I would take the new students and show them how to walk deliberately. Starting very slowly we would concentrate on the action of walking, shifting our balance and weight onto the leading leg, rotating out hips, bringing the following leg forward, placing the weight and balance forward etc.

Once I had the class doing this for ten minutes or so and their concentration was one hundred percent I would then ask them to think about their breathing at the same time. In some cases this was literally too much for some people to handle and they would either stop walking completely, as they found thinking about these two things at the same time was too much information or, some would just fall flat on their faces! You may well laugh, I've seen it happen.

What I'm trying to say here is that walking does not require much thought as we do it automatically. (There are rumours that certain politicians cannot walk and chew gum at the same time but that's an old joke.) Where our mind can benefit from walking is in that it is free to not have to think. When I walk I allow my mind to wander, to rest, to play, perhaps to dream. And like I said before, sometimes our best ideas are born in this time. I balance myself in all three areas. My body is being exercised for which I feel better emotionally and my mind is left to plan the rest of my day, what a bonus! And when I then get back to work, I work at a higher level than when I stopped to go for a walk – double bonus!

1.14 Moderate exercise

Moderate exercise must be strenuous but not overwhelming. We must be able to push ourselves just beyond what is known as our optimum limit. To understand this further it is necessary to explain increased heart rates and their function. Our cardiovascular system (heart and lungs) is a very fine instrument that is specifically designed to respond to the changing needs of our bodies at different times. When we rest our breathing and heart rates are very low because our muscles will only demand the right amount of oxygen for them to function. If our muscles are relaxed so is our cardiovascular system.

When we move from the resting state and engage in any form of movement our muscles require more oxygen and so our heart beats faster in order to supply more oxygen rich blood to the parts that are now in greater need. This will have an immediate effect on other biochemical levels in our bodies such as blood sugars, lactic acid, adrenaline, endorphin and serotonin production etc. This will create the causes for other long term effects, such as increased blood flow to the skin, resulting in a more youthful complexion, improved muscle tone and the like. Consequently we will look and feel a whole lot better in ourselves in that we also gain those inevitable spin off benefits such as strengthening in our minds and emotions.

As has been proven many times, the more exercise we do the healthier our bodies become, and so, the more exercise we can do the more we generate an upward spiral of benefits. Remember that our bodies are designed to do work. I often think when I see labourers performing such hard and demanding physical work "My God! There's no way that I could sustain that amount of physical work". So how do they do it? Do they go to special labourers training camp and subject their bodies to a regime of heavy exercise in order to 'pass' and so become labourers? Of course not, they just do plenty of it until their bodies can sustain that amount of regular physical activity. And let's face it; all labourers are not exactly built like Arnold Schwarzenegger are they? All they have done is worked with their bodies on or around their optimum limit for a lot longer than the majority of us. And although the human body is an amazing machine one fact remains, it is not inexhaustible. Even a fit labourer could not sustain too long a period of working beyond their optimal limit, it's simply impossible. So we must all find our optimum limit in order to progress. This is when we have exercised to our own (and nobody else's) limit and cannot and therefore should not do any more. Our optimum limit is purely subjective and differs from each individual. One thing to do is to measure your heart rate when exercising against these tables:

Figure 4 : Heart Rate for Exercise

Age	Beginner 60-70%		Intermediate 70-80%		Advanced 80-90%	
	Beats/min	Beats/10Sec	Beats/min	Beats/10Sec	Beats/min	Beats/10Sec
to 19	121-141	20 - 24	141-161	24 - 27	161-181	27 - 30
20 - 24	119-139	20 - 23	139-158	23 - 26	158-178	26 - 30
25 - 29	116-135	19 - 23	135-154	23 - 26	154-178	26 - 29
30 - 34	113-132	19 - 22	132-150	22 - 25	150-169	25 - 28
35 - 39	110-128	18 - 21	128-146	21 - 24	146-165	24 - 28
40 - 44	107-125	18 - 21	125-142	21 - 24	142-160	24 - 27
45 - 49	104-121	17 - 20	121-138	20 - 23	138-156	23 - 26
50 - 54	101-118	17 - 20	118-134	20 - 22	134-151	22 - 25
55 - 59	98-114	16 - 19	114-130	19 - 22	130-147	22 - 25
60 - 64	95-111	16 - 19	111-126	19 - 21	126-142	21 - 24
65 - 69	92-107	15 - 18	107-122	18 - 20	122-138	20 - 23
70 - 74	89-104	15 - 17	104-118	17 - 20	118-133	20 - 22
75 - 79	86-100	14 - 17	100-114	17 - 19	114-129	19 - 22
80 - 84	83-97	14 - 16	97-110	16 - 18	110-124	18 - 21
85+	81-95	14 - 16	95-108	16 - 18	108-122	18 - 20

To measure your heart rate the best method is to place two fingers onto you carotid artery (at the side of the throat) and count the number of beats in ten seconds and simply multiply this by six. This is your heart rate. Depending on your age group you can then tell if you are working within or beyond your boundaries. This is the most crucial element in sustaining any long-term exercise program.

Here is one of the classic success/failure cycles that people go through. They exercise with a passion. Their mind is set of looking and feeling good. A great way to start but, unfortunately, they simply overdo it. They train like someone possessed, they enrol in the gyms, they book aerobics classes and within two weeks they are completely exhausted. Their eagerness is greater than their ability so of course their bodies react, usually with the classic signs of pain and aching muscles. Remember, pain is our body's natural response that tells us that we should stop. They have no choice but to listen to this pain and consequently, not only do they put off the next exercise routine, but worst of all things, they associate exercise with pain and inevitably give up! Sounds familiar? How sad. Their enthusiasm now plummets to an all time low along with their emotional state and the next time they decide to do something about it the harder and harder it becomes. Remember two things; one, we are not as young as we were and two, we are never going to be as young as we are right now, so try and balance the two.

So, once we have sustained this optimum limit for no more than a few times, our heart and lungs will be used to being pushed to this point and therefore will be more able to sustain greater amounts of exercise, but again to an optimal point. No person can train, train and train again. Part of our biological function is to rest so that we may recuperate as our muscles need time to restructure to enable a greater flow of oxygen for next time we exercise. A good rule of thumb is only to perform moderate exercise every other day. Light exercises every day, moderate exercise every other and enjoy! Enjoy finding your limits and playing with them. Listen to your body as it will tell you when it's time to speed up and when it's time to slow down.

1.15 Swimming

An ideal example of moderate exercise is swimming, as it is one of the only forms of activity that exercises all the main muscle groups together without punishing them. It's also a great form of exercise for anyone suffering from some form of physical injury. Why do you think that most hospitals now have pools for hydrotherapy? It's also become very popular for expectant mothers to do aqua-natal classes. Have you also noticed the emergence of aqua-aerobics? This is because water and especially exercising in water, has been recognised, dating as far back as the Roman era, as being highly beneficial.

I used swimming as my primary therapy when I was recovering from a serious operation on my spine. I was informed that swimming is the best form of exercise for a core body muscles, specifically around the length of the back bone, and by strengthening these muscles I would be giving my spinal column the best support possible.

When you first begin to swim you should only do as many lengths as you can and no more. That may be three, five, ten, or even one length. Don't worry; these targets are yours and yours alone. If you can't swim then the primary reason is simply that you have not learned to do so, so learn. Some people cannot swim, or more precisely have chosen to convince themselves that they cannot swim out of some fear or phobia. Remember, as we will discuss in more detail later, fears and phobias are blockages in our emotional centre that can, and should, be resolved. And think how much better you'll feel when you've been able to overcome these. All you have to do is, you've guessed it, try! Also, if you feel in bad shape then just imagine how much better you will feel when you can double or treble your own 'personal best' and as every athlete will tell you, it is breaking your own 'PB' that gives you the greatest sense of achievement. Like with walking you must also record your times as these will also increase, along with your confidence, as you get quicker and quicker and so another virtuous circle begins.

Your Guru is the best person to give you a pat on the back. They will be there, clipboard in hand, charting your progress and although they are strict they are also quick to give praise when it's due. Also your Guru will not be too hard on you so don't be too hard on yourself. As you listen to your body more and more you will hear when it says 'slow down'. Although I maintain a regular exercise routine there are times when, for whatever reason, it could be that my blood sugars are low or my electrolyte levels are in imbalance, I just have to either slow down or do less distance. Remember that you don't always have to better your personal best. This is a target that can only be achieved every now and then so it is important to recognise and honour your personal energy cycles and accept that you may well be energetic one day, or at a particular time of day, and not so much the next.

Let me just add a word of warning to anyone suffering from a spinal condition, as well as problems with the knees and hips. Breaststroke, although the easiest, is actually the worst stroke that you could be doing. The reason being is that your are continually bending and straightening your back that could and almost certainly will aggravate or even exacerbate the problem. There is also the possibility of potential damage to the hips, as they are being pushed laterally away from the body, injuries will only be aggravated. As for the knees, breaststroke is the worst ever. The knee is designed to move in one direction, up and down, and not side to side as they tend to do when doing this stoke. Front-crawl however, in all these applications, is a far better form of moderate exercise in that it puts no unnecessary stress and strains on those parts. When I first began to use swimming as therapy I primarily swam breaststroke as I was unable to do more than one length of front crawl without coughing and spluttering and feeling totally exhausted. So all I did was alternate, one breaststroke, and one front crawl. Then I'd do sets of threes. Front crawl, breaststroke and then front crawl again. Then I moved on to sevens until I was able to do three lengths of front crawl, then seven and eventually three lots of seven. This took me nearly three years to do, so be patient; you've got the rest of your life to work on this. Consequently I find myself in my mid-forties and getting fitter and fitter every year where most of my contemporaries are just getting fatter and fatter.

Remember, during any moderate exercise you should only be pushing yourself to your optimum limit. It is not designed to do you more damage. So, be sensible and listen to your body. If you find that you get an excessive amount of pain after training, then find a stroke that is easier for you. Backstroke is also a great all round stroke, so long as your shoulders are fine.

Swimming also gives your mind the time to quieten down. Some people say that swimming is boring, but most find it extremely restful. If you find the prospect of length after length unappealing then try this. Dedicate your swimming to someone else! After each length, turn and in your mind say "I dedicate this length to…" Now, that could be to your lover, as you will be fitter, to a long lost friend who would certainly love to be able to swim with you, to a Master so that you can be your best, to a student, so that you can do your best. Dedicate it to your mother in thanks for being born, the list is as endless and as varied as you want to make it. By the way, you are also allowed to dedicate it to yourself, and your Guru.

As your exercise programme expands you will come to realise that the more complex the exercise the more you move towards balance in body, mind and soul. All three centres will begin to work in unison. As your physical centre takes exercise you will inevitably feel a whole lot better in your emotional centre. And as your intellect takes note of your timings it will notice an obvious improvement and therefore rationally validate your actions and so this becomes another virtuous circle. Your mind says it's good, your body knows it's good and your emotions confirm it all and consequently the more you want, and will be more able, to do.

1.16 Yoga

There is no greater example of this blending of mind, body and soul (excepting some Martial Arts) than Yoga. Yoga is one of the oldest forms of total exercise known to mankind; experts date it to as far back as 5,000BC. The therapeutic benefits of Yoga have long been recognised as it not only exercises all the main muscle groups, it also exercises the whole skeletal structure and our organs, as well as the mind. One of the initial benefits is that you will certainly find that your cardiovascular capacity will be much improved, resulting in your muscles being able to sustain more exercise. It's quite simple, the more you do the more you will be able to do but don't give up! Yoga is initially very hard for most of us in the West as we will be exercising parts of our bodies that not only have we not done so for a long time, but also that we didn't even know existed! You must accept the fact that there will be aches and pains but try to congratulate yourself that you are making the changes that are for your long-term good.

Accepting the fact that there are many different forms of Yoga, which usually depends on the region it was first developed in, the basic rules of Yoga in terms of mind, body and soul do tend to remain the same. Yoga, in fact, was initially developed as a system specifically designed to augment an extreme religious practice. It was designed to enable devotees to purify themselves in order for them to reach a point of enlightenment in their meditations. That's why so many Yoga classes include relaxation techniques alongside strenuous physical exercises.

The Yogi's believe that the three aspects of mind body and soul are also inextricably linked. One cannot separate one from the other. If you exercise your body you can, and must, exercise your mind and spirit at the same time. We've already looked into the link between exercise and well being but Yoga turns this into a pure science. Take for instance the healing properties of the mind. We are all familiar with the concept of the placebo effect where countless studies have documented and proven that the mind has as much of an effect on our bodies healing as do conventional or alternative, medicines. In short, if we believe we are going to be cured we stand a far greater chance that we will be than if we believe that we will not.

The very cornerstone of Yoga is underpinned by this fact; the mind can have dominance over the body. Have you ever seen one of these Yoga Mystics put spikes through their skin or lie on a bed of nails? How can they do this? Simply because they have developed, through their practice, the ability to put their 'mind over matter'. I'm not for a moment suggesting that we should all sharpen our Kebab spikes and try this out, what I'm saying is that if the mind is that powerful how can we turn that to our advantage? After all the difference in one highly trained sports person and the next usually lies in their belief. Why do you think that most successful sportsmen and women have personal Positive Mental Attitude instructors? The answer is because it works and it is often the difference between gold and an 'also ran'.

When choosing the style of Yoga that suits you best take a few test-drives. Go along to various classes and find which method, and in a lot of cases which teacher, you will be able to work best with. This is probably the most defining factor when choosing your Yoga class as it is virtually impossible to learn Yoga by any other way. It would be a bit like reading a book on how to swim and all the Positive Mental Attitude in convincing yourself that you can swim will lead to nothing when you finally hit the water! Your teacher is essential in being able to show you, through years of direct experience, the way for you to get the best out of your studies. Some styles concentrate more on the body whilst others concentrate more on relaxation of the mind. Some teachers are old, some are young, some more physical, some more cerebral. Find the one that suits you best.

In summary, moderate exercise should ideally not occur every day as your cardiovascular system, as well as your muscles, needs time to recover. You should aim to do moderate exercise every other day. Other forms of moderate exercise can be prolonged brisk walking, cycling, dancing and sex (which for some is the most enjoyable form of exercise!).

Once, and only then, you have been able to sustain moderate exercise for around twenty-five to thirty minutes you will be able to move to the hardest form of all, heavy exercise. However, it is worth remembering here that it is far better to rotate between light and moderate exercise over and over again before attempting any form of heavy exercise even if this takes years. Remember your Guru is you and if it doesn't feel right don't feel forced into it. A Guru will only give you the best advice (but don't allow this to be an excuse to be lazy!).

1.17 Heavy exercise

Heavy exercise can be categorised into what I term 'grunting and spitting'. Again there are many forms of heavy exercise to choose from, and again, you must decide which is best for you. Your local gymnasium is sure to offer a wide variety of courses from working out in the gym or fitness room to aerobics, martial arts, boxing, circuit training and the like.

Heavy exercise does not mean going to the gym and on the very first session trying to lift the heaviest weights possible. It's all about working just beyond your optimum limit and most importantly of all only just beyond. As you begin to do more and more repetitions you will then be able to sustain heavy exercise for longer and longer periods. Bear this in mind, if you overdo it you will suffer. Your body will ache in unknown places and again you will associate exercise with pain and not want to do it. However, heavy exercise is about maintaining your own individual pain barrier and experimenting with it. By experimenting with it I mean holding that pain threshold for as long as possible without causing any actual physical damage.

When you are grunting and spitting you are in fact going against what your body is trying to tell you. What it's trying to say is "Stop!" However, if you have already conditioned your body through the process of rotating light and moderate exercise then you will be more able to push yourself in heavy exercise to the point just beyond when your body is screaming out to stop. Don't worry too much as your body, more exactly your muscles, will only be able to sustain shorts bursts as the lactic acid that is a bi-product of extreme muscle usage will build up and prevent overuse.

Remember to make sure that you drink plenty of fluids because when performing heavy exercise your body will heat up quite dramatically and you will certainly sweat a lot more if you are doing it right. Remember, heavy exercise can only be sustained in short bursts. So, push yourself and then stop and rest for a while, until you have at the very least got your breath back then push yourself once more. You will find as your performance increases you will be able to rest for shorter periods and push for longer.

If you don't have a personal trainer remember that you are your own best trainer. You know what your limits are and you will know when to speed up or slow down. Again, imagine your own personal training Guru is stood behind you, clipboard in hand, marking your progress, giving you advice and encouragement and offering congratulations on a job well done. Don't forget that nowadays it is common that in most gyms you will be taken through an induction programme (some even insist on you seeking medical advice) before given an exercise programme and then given a chart to mark your progress.

Power walking is also an excellent form of heavy exercise as it is something we are all familiar with and it's really cheap too! Just make sure you have got suitable footwear and don't try to do too much. Most army fitness training is predominately based on marching, power walking is the basis of all marching, but you don't have to do it with a sergeant major screaming at you. Find your own pace and do as much as you can, and the next time just do a little bit more.

Other forms of heavy exercise include running, football, sprint swimming, martial arts, boxing, Aerobics, squash etc. The list is as limited as your imagination and your application. All you have to do is keep searching until you find the one, or ones, you enjoy the most. Then, in the words of a famous sporting designer label, 'Just Do It!'

1.18 Gym

Have you noticed the emergence of the 'super gyms'? All over the place fitness centres are springing up and offering all kinds of courses. When you go into these places they are filled with a whole plethora of equipment ranging from running machines to weight training equipment. There seems to be a machine for every different muscle in the body, such is their variety.

It is as though being fit and keeping fit is the latest craze to sweep through the country. I think it's down to another reason all together as crazes invariably die out. I think it is due to the fact that because we live in the information age and so much knowledge on the workings of the body is readily available that most people are aware of the fact that exercise is essential in maintaining balance in our everyday lives. We live longer and fuller lives and the growth in leisure activities is one of life's, and businesses, constants. We are all becoming more aware of how exercise and diet is good for us and so in great numbers we are enrolling in these many classes. For our parent's generation it was completely different and most illnesses and deaths could certainly be put down to mere ignorance. We, however, have no such excuses. We know that, for instance, smoking is harmful, but not so long ago smoking was recommended by doctors for stress relief as little was known about the effects of tar and nicotine.

A good gym should be able to offer you an exercise programme that suits you best as they have trained instructors who are there to offer you professional advice as to what is best for your individual needs, but try to bear these basic requirements in mind.

Always try to structure an exercise programme that will give your body a complete workout. By this I mean that it must be varied in, not only the muscle groups that you exercise but also a combination of both aerobic and anaerobic exercise. Aerobic exercise usually tends to concentrate on getting your cardiovascular system working over longer and more sustained periods, whereas anaerobic exercise tends to be muscular exercise in shorts bursts. For instance when you start any form of exercise you are always recommended to warm up so that your heart and lungs will be able to supply enough oxygen rich blood to your muscles so that they may operate at maximum efficiency, as well as ensuring that you don't injure yourself. This is aerobic exercise.

Once you have warmed up on a stepper or a cycling or rowing machine you have kick started your cardiovascular system into action, this can now sustain a burst of anaerobic exercise. So move onto one of the weight machines and complete those repetitions. This should then be followed by another burst of aerobic exercise and so on. Always try to alternate aerobic and anaerobic exercise until you can do no more, warm down, then rest and take on plenty of fluids. These will not only replace lost fluids but also cleanse your system of all the nasty bi-products of exercising (build-ups of lactic acid and the like.) It's a bit like having an oil change after every race and let's face it, for a racing car to work at its maximum efficiency they are always treated with the best of care and attention. (More will be discussed later when we discuss diet.)

1.19 Aerobics

Another huge trend in exercise programmes is the emergence of Aerobics classes. One of the greatest assets of this is down to the fact that we are exercising with other people. Usually exercise is limited to what we do on our own, even if that is at a gym with dozens of other people as we are all doing our own individual routine (or plugged into our iPods!) with the odd nod or wink to someone just passing by. Exercise doesn't have to be this way as one of the main reasons why some people don't exercise at all is because they find it boring whereas the company of others can be very stimulating. It all depends on what you are most comfortable with. Some people don't want anyone else around and work better in isolation whilst others thrive on company; it's merely a matter of personal preference.

Don't forget that we are social animals and are used to working in groups, so working out in groups is a natural extension of that. Aerobics classes often become like social events where we are able to get away from the kids or the job and go out with our friends. Most classes tend to spill over into sharing refreshments at the end and so on. Also most people tend to join a new class on the recommendation of a friend in the first place.

Again, before choosing a class that best suits you try a few beforehand to check out the atmosphere, the teacher and probably most importantly of all, the level of fitness of the class. You don't want to be joining a class that is too far advanced for you if you are just beginning as this can be counterproductive for a number of reasons. Firstly, you have to learn to walk before you can run, but also there is nothing worse than feeling like the worst or slowest or the least fit in the class as this will lead to inevitable demoralisation and that's the last thing you need when just starting out. It's always best to find a class that is equivalent to your own abilities because again if you overdo it in the early stages you will inevitably associate exercise with pain, or worse still, cringing embarrassment, and probably give up.

Remember your Guru in you will ultimately know what is best for you and what isn't. This is not down to the standards of others. They can only advise; it is you that must apply. Unfortunately this is one of the common pitfalls of group exercising as the standards are set by others, so if you choose to exercise this way then try to err on the side of caution, always find your own standard and never give up! If it's not working for you then remember that you are free to quit (but I don't mean forever!), there is no shame in recognising your strengths and weaknesses, far from it, as you can always find another class that is more suited to your individual requirements. This inner wisdom can take you to any place you wish to go and can also give you the ability to decide where not to go. This is not failure, it is success in another guise and it will put you on another route to your eventual long-term fitness, happiness and sense of fulfilment and balance. Your Guru in you is the best judge of this, listen to them, let them decide and then act. Eventually, through a process of trial and error, you will find a system that best suits you and gives sufficient evidence to prove that you are progressing and any progress is worth encouragement, and the more encouraged you are the greater the virtuous circle turns in your favour.

1.20 Martial Arts

This is one of my most favourite subjects and I could rattle on about it until the cows come home, but I won't as I could certainly write a whole book on the vastness of this particular topic. Martial Arts are as individual as fingerprints and an almost confusing array of styles are available from which to choose from to find the one that will suit you best. My own particular style is Ninjutsu which says this as its basic premise; we are all built different, we walk different, we talk different, some are young, some are old, some are fit, some are not. So how can two moves be the same? What works for one person will not work for the next. As long as the end result is the same what difference does it make to what technique we use?

If you decide that you wish to try to practice a Martial Art you must be ready to embark on an external quest of learning as Martial Arts transcend the mere physical and moves us into another realm altogether. A realm where your three centres are working in perfect unison. You will not just be exercising your body but also your mind and emotions. All Martial Artists will tell you that after a while the practising of techniques becomes secondary to the whole. Techniques are merely physical repetitions that eventually teach your body and mind that you know how to do that particular technique and work towards perfection. Ah, that elusive thing called perfection. It has often been said that the pursuit of perfection is not a destination; it is a journey of self-discovery. Reaching perfection is like attaining enlightenment, that's where it all begins; it's not where it all ends.

The best way to find a Martial Art that suits you is first to observe your body. How are you built? Are you fast or powerful? Are you agile or rigid? Are you hard like steel or springier like willow? Observing your body will point you in the right direction for finding a style that works for you, all you then have to do is shop around. Look in the local paper to see what classes are being held and go along to a few before you decide. And again, like with Yoga and Aerobics, it is often the choice of teacher that will finally make up your mind for you. In Martial Arts there is no stronger relationship than that between Master and Student. You must find a Master who you have utmost respect and admiration for if you are going to be able to learn anything at all. Very often we tend to choose like minded or like spirited people. Some prefer their Masters to be loud and aggressive whilst others prefer the Master who lives by the motto: *tread softly and talk with a quiet voice.* Ultimately you, and your Guru in you, must decide. Don't be afraid to ask questions as the right teacher will see that you posses an enquiring mind and relish the opportunity of teaching you. If, on the other hand, they are evasive it's usually because they have got something to hide so the best thing to do is simply walk away until you find someone who can answer your questions.

Practising Martial Arts is not about learning to beat people up, far from it. It is in fact about learning how to protect all living beings, not just yourself. However there is certainly something very comforting in having the ability to defend yourself in a threatening situation, this is self-empowerment in action. You know that in most cases harm will not come to you and by banishing fear we become liberated. Consequently we are more confident, more able and less threatening to others. Most people only ever get into physical confrontations because someone else has found them to be a threat and so conflict arises. When you don't threaten you tend not to get into conflict.

People often ask the old question, "Have you ever had to use your Martial Arts?" as they wish to hear of stories where you are leaping around like Bruce Lee seeing off all comers. I answer, "Yes, all the time". By this I mean that every time that I haven't got into a fight is because I've used my skills to avoid physical confrontation. This is beyond the physical and by definition becomes metaphysical, of the mind. I use my confidence or humbleness, to avoid a situation before it starts, this is the truest way of using Martial Arts, and it's easier to run than to fight.

Some of you may be thinking "Well what's the point in learning something that you will never need to use?" That's a bit like asking "Why should I learn First-Aid?" Or "Why do I need insurance?" It's always best to be covered and sometimes we have to learn things that we hope to never have to use. Studying Martial Arts is a lesson in humility and can open up many aspects of our lives we never dreamed possible like patience, tolerance and respect. These are valuable lessons indeed and prerequisites for living a fully balanced and rounded existence. Give it a try; I'm sure that you will be pleasantly surprised.

Some of you, like me, may well be pacifists and totally opposed to any and all forms of violence and therefore not wish to take up Martial Arts in the mistaken belief that you are somehow engaging in violence, this could not be farther from the truth. Martial Arts are all about self-preservation not violence and there are plenty of 'soft' styles that may well suit you better. Tai Chi for instance is still classified as a Martial Art but you will never come across a more graceful example of beauty in movement. Some of the other Chinese styles are almost like a ballet in their grace of execution. They are a real pleasure to perform and to observe and may well tap depths within yourself that you never knew existed.

Tai Chi comes from Tai, meaning movement, and Chi, meaning the energy that flows through all things. Literally it means the movement of one's Chi. To explain Chi in a few words is not only impossible but also disrespectful to those who have made it a science and I will not attempt to slander their teachings with my own explanation. Part of self-discovery is just that, you must discover this for yourselves. However, more will be discussed about Chi in the section on Acupuncture.

DIET

Food consumption is directly proportional to the amount of available energy we can use. The less ones food intake the less energy we have and if we don't feed an engine with the correct fuel we can never build up a good head of steam. Imagine putting wet logs on a fire or coal that has been soaked in water. What are we going to achieve? First of all it's definitely going to be difficult to light, if at all. The furnace of our physical body is no different. It can only work efficiently when it has been topped up with the right kind of fuel. Our bodies are like engines and think about what happens if you accidentally fill up a car that runs on petrol with diesel? It simply doesn't work.

The same is true with our bodies. If we don't give it the right fuel it will not work for us. We don't run on gasoline, nor do we live on grass! Much is now understood about maintaining a properly nutritionally balanced diet and we are all much more aware of the importance of reducing our consumption of foods with high fat and sugar content as well as processed foods.

I happen to like the phrase by Oscar Wilde which states *"Everything in moderation, except moderation itself"* which to me means that we must be careful as to what we do, but not to the point of being obsessed. We all know plenty of people who are always on some kind of diet or other or some kind of magic cure-all supplement, to the point that their lives are led by one fad after the other, depending upon what is fashionable at the time and unfortunately most of our diets and eating habits are primarily media and celebrity influenced. Such-and-such uses this diet therefore it must be good. Or, so-and-so recommended this and she/he looks great.

Our physical appearance is all too often governed by mass media influence which has undoubtedly resulted in countless dietary and eating disorders. Where is it written that all women must be a size eight and be slim? In every magazine, advert, film, and most TV programmes that's where! Even men are now pressured by the 'body beautiful' and a 'six pack' stomach is now considered as some kind of must-have fashion accessory. It is little wonder why so many people are desperately unhappy about their appearance because the media says that if we are not good looking enough, then we are simply not good enough, full stop.

As with exercise you must first find a diet that works for you and not some diet or fad that others say you should have. You must also define the look of YOUR OWN BODY because that is what it is, your body, no one else's. Nobody chooses their body from a catalogue, (cosmetic surgery aside) so you have to make the most of the hand that you have been dealt. There will always be something about your appearance that you are unhappy with or that irritates you and the fact of the matter is that all you can do is live with it and get on. Instead of complaining about those things that you are unhappy with about your body why not concentrate on being proud of what you have got and those simple things that you can do like walking, talking, seeing, smelling, touching, feeling and tasting?

Face it; as long as our senses are unimpaired everything else is a bonus. I think we all spend too much time missing what we haven't got rather than appreciating what we have. This is an unfortunate and insidious tendency in most people's lives, which we simply have to change if we are going to stand up and feel proud of our bodies and in turn feel proud of ourselves.

So, what action is necessary in order for us to feel proud with our bodies? My mother, who is now in her early seventies, has practiced yoga for nearly forty years and has an interesting expression when talking about pride in ones appearance. She says "If you can stand naked in front of the mirror and not feel ashamed, then you can do anything." Exercise and diet are the cornerstones for us to be able to feel this way and a nutritionally balanced diet is essential for us to be able to sustain any prolonged physical exercise programme, ask any athlete. I know that when I have an extremely busy work schedule and I do not put enough time aside in order to train regularly or if I don't eat as well as I ought to then I actually begin to feel my life-force reducing in discernible increments. Then when I am able to get back into my regular exercise programme and diet my life force increases as does my equilibrium, enthusiasm, and performance resultant benefits. In short, I am more balanced and I maximise my potential.

When we feed ourselves correctly we perform better, simple. This in turn has a direct impact on the way we feel about ourselves, and when we feel better about ourselves, we perform better. It's a virtuous circle. The better we feel the better we do, and the better we do, the better we feel.

1.21 Diet not Dieting

What is the difference between a diet and dieting? Well a diet is something that we all have regardless of conscious effort. We eat the foods we have always eaten and pay little or no regard to their nutritional, fat or sugar content. To diet, or to go on a diet, is to make a conscious effort to watch and understand the foods that we eat. The difference lies purely in our consciousness. When we engage our consciousness we embark on a journey of discovery. We set sail to new and unfamiliar territories and like travel; we broaden our horizons and bring variety into our lives. When we learn anything new then its effects can be both subtle and profound. When we try foods that we have never tried before, we experience and in doing so we learn.

We learn what we like and dislike, what suits us and what doesn't, what agrees with us and what we prefer to avoid. At this point we must remember the old analogy of our mind being like a parachute; it only works when it's open! Try not to close your mind as to what you think you might like until you've tried it in the first place then, and only then, will you be able to apply direct experience to find what you truly like and dislike. Here's the main point to consider. Very few people can guarantee that their diet is completely balanced 100% as there is always room for improvement. Once you accept this fact then you will continuously find improvement. Let's face it; there are such a wide variety of foods from around the world, which are readily available, that you could spend a lifetime trying out all these wonderful dishes (what a lovely thought).

Food is such a sensual experience as it taps into our basic hierarchy of needs (warmth, clothes and shelter being the others). We, on the whole, all love our foods as we engage most of our senses in the act of eating. We hear the dish being prepared, we smell it, we see the dish in our bowl or decorating our plate, we touch it (either with our mouths or our fingers and mouths) and we taste it and, occasionally, let out sounds akin to orgasm! (Incidentally, one of the reasons that we tend to clink our glasses together when raising a toast is that it engages our sense of hearing.) All our senses play their part in deciding whether or not we like it and any one of them can make us decide if we want to try it again.

A rich variety is essential to stop us becoming bored with our food, which, when you really think about it is a very strange, luxurious concept, only available in rich countries where food is like any other commodity. You will rarely find people in poor countries complaining about being bored with their diet, they simply eat what they can to survive. But because we live in a society where we have the choice as to what we eat then, like exercise, we must choose what we like. We must consciously explore our likes and dislikes and find a diet that is both nutritious as well as interesting. If we do this then we need never diet again. We can rise above the whims of a fickle industry and find our own perfect weight, shape and size. We will feel, look and live better.

Your energy output is directly linked to your energy input. This is one of the irrefutable laws of nature. You cannot get more out than you put in. So, if you eat low energy foods, your energy will be low. If you eat a lot of processed foods, which are let's face it 'dead', then how do you think you will feel? You must consider your body and treat it as though it is a finely tuned engine or machine and look what happens if you treat any machine in a bad way. If your car never had an oil change do you think that it would work at its optimum level? Of course not, our bodies are no different. They need regular servicing and maintenance.

So, how do we go about doing this? Here are a few tips, gleaned from years of experience and practice in trial and error.

1.22 Bad Habits

Have you ever noticed how easy it is to create a bad eating habit and stick to it, rather than to establish a good eating habit and continue with it? With all the 'convenience foods' and 'fast foods' that are available to us it is hardly surprising is it? Everywhere we go we are bombarded with fast food franchises which serve us with food, which we know is often not nutritious as well as expensive, but still we choose to eat it, why is that? It's basically laziness, nothing more nothing less. In this day and age when we have more food and a far greater variety of foods than at any other time in human history, why do we do it? You only have to talk to older people, particularly those who lived through the war, about their diets and what was available to them to realise that we have a far greater choice than they ever did yet the nutritional balance of their diet was often far greater than ours. For instance, the growth rate of obesity in Western society is proportionately linked to the increase in fast food consumption. In some cases people have actually tried to sue some of these fast food companies for making their food so addictive. It's as if they are being marched into these places against their will and force-fed!

This attitude is typical of the blame culture where people will only blame the actions of others rather than take responsibility for their own actions. I don't know about you but I've never seen anyone dragged into one of these fast food restaurants against their will. I've never seen people press ganged kicking and screaming and forced to sit down and eat, have you? (Except maybe some unruly children) Of course not, We all, willingly, queue up and pay for the latest designer label Mega-Meal and then sit through the cheesy piped music and the sound of children screaming to 'enjoy' our meal.

It's all so easy to fall for these traps because the ad-men say that unless we eat at these places we are somehow socially excluded what nonsense! It's all about taking responsibility for our own actions and understanding the consequences of those actions. Don't get me wrong, I'm not saying that we shouldn't eat at these places at all, just don't make it all the time. Anyone that has got children will testify that it's often the most convenient way of keeping the kids quiet when out on a shopping trip. The problem then becomes that it is a must do thing. It's like stuffing our faces with popcorn and fizzy drinks when we go to watch a film at the cinema. Everybody does it. We sit there, transfixed, probably not even noticing that we are doing it. Why is that? Does it help with our level of concentration? I don't think so. Does it increase our level of enjoyment? To answer that question next time you go to watch a movie don't eat and see what you think. As I did, you'll probably find that it doesn't spoil your enjoyment one iota, but you will find yourself wondering why everyone is stuffing their faces without even knowing it.

The reason why we do it is simple, it's a habit, and the problem with any bad habit is that we don't even know we are doing it until someone else points it out. From now on what I want you to do is to become aware of your eating habits and try to categorise it as what you would consider as either good or bad. But here's the fun bit, you get to decide what your own definition of what is good or bad. Use your own wisdom and then decide. So for instance, if you enjoy pizza for example it would be wrong to say that eating pizza is bad. However if you eat pizza and nothing else then surely this cannot be good can it? When judging your diet remember that, as with everything else in life, balance is the most important thing of all. Try to remember that to have a balanced diet you should eat foods from all the main food groups (carbohydrates, protein, fats, vitamins, fibre, water and minerals) and to increase your consumption of fresh fruits and vegetables as well as increasing your water intake. By analysing your diet you get a good understanding of what you eat most of and what you eat the least of and if you see particular trends then you are in a far better position to do something about it.

It's so easy to create a bad eating habit but the good news is it's also very easy to create a good eating habit. It's like any other habit, the more we enforce it the more ingrained it becomes. Also, like any other habit, it has been proven that it will take around 24 days for us to make or break it, in some cases it can be longer or shorter depending on how deep the habit is. For instance, if you smoke 60 a day cigarettes then it will probably take you longer to kick the habit than someone who smokes 10 a day.

It's no surprise that as the level of incidence and vast variety of eating disorders increases the level of our collective health decreases as the two go hand in hand. There's a lot of truth in the old adage 'you are what you eat' and if you want to remain dull and sluggish then carry on eating dull food. If you want to remain lifeless then eat lifeless food. But on the other hand if you want your life energy to increase then eat food with more life energy in it like fruit and vegetables. If you want to remain healthy then eat food which will create those benefits, but remember, no one else is going to do it for you! No one else can take responsibility for your eating habits, only you. But I urge you to change your mind set. Try not to think of this as some dreary task to be completed because if you do you will soon fall back to the path of lazy eating. Instead try to consider it as a gift that you are giving yourself. To put it another way, you could do it if your life depended on it couldn't you? But in a very real sense it does. Your quality of life is directly linked to your diet, so if you want to increase your quality of life you must increase the quality of your diet; it's a simple as that! (That doesn't mean it has to be dull either. We will consider this in greater detail when we discuss variety.)

1.23 Nutrition

This is like one of those subjects at school where we thought, "Oh no. Not this again". This seems to be one of those topics that most people skip over as if the only ones it should concern are the biologists and nutritionists, how wrong. Nutrition affects each and every one of us just as the sun affects each and every living being, for without either we could simply not exist. We are biological creatures that are products of our environments. We are, quite literally, what we eat. To understand this we must explore our biological function in relation to the environment.

Original energy comes in the form of light from the Sun shining, plants absorb this energy and through the process of photosynthesis grow, we eat the plants, and the animals that feed on those plants and in turn directly convert that original energy into energy for our bodies. We are creatures of light. Without light the whole cycle would simply grind to a halt. Now there are some that have convinced themselves that they can live on light alone, but to paraphrase, 'man cannot live on bread alone', we must have variety to ensure a nutritionally balanced diet.

We used to consider that the word 'Malnutrition' was something limited to third world countries where images of children standing on spindly legs with painfully distended bellies comes to mind, this is not so. The World Health Organisation recently produced results that confirm that nearly half the population of the western world now has a diet that is so replete in nutrition it can therefore be classified as malnourished. Our modern day diet of processed and fatty food does not give us a fully balanced and nutritional diet; it's as simple as that! Recently I read an article stating that some hospitals run 'constipation clinics' for children who have not passed a stool for weeks due to the high levels of fat and sugar in their diets and the low levels of fibre, how sad this is? But why is it so? We have at our disposal a far greater variety of foods than at any other time in mankind's history. We also have a far greater understanding of nutrition and the direct correlation with our health. So, in effect, we are deliberately choosing an unhealthy diet. Why do we do this? The answer is, yet again, that it is easier that way, basically we are lazy! It's a sad fact that it is far easier to microwave some chips than it is to peel a potato.

However, the product of our own laziness has far reaching implications to the health of our children. Because it's easier to feed kids on junk food we take the easy option and do so. Because our kids have grown accustomed to fish fingers, chicken nuggets, burgers and beans it's almost impossible to change their bad eating habits because, as every parent knows, you can't force them to eat something they don't like. There's also no point dishing out threats like 'If you don't eat your dinner you won't get any pudding', it's far too late for that. It's a rod made for your own back, it is the consequences of the actions you have taken but, there is some good news. Like any bad habit, it can be changed; again it's just a matter of time.

If you seriously want to take responsibility for your own nutritional health, and for that of your children, you have to make the conscious decision to change, but to do it gradually. A decision to change can be made in an instant; but the results of that change of attitude will invariably take longer to actualise. However, that does not mean you should become complacent and lazy. Determine to make a change and then stick to it. Know that the good causes you are making in the present will have good effects in the long run. We all take responsibility for the health of our children, yet why would we want to harm our children's long term health by depriving them of 'proper' food? When changing your children's diet remember that gradual change is better than radical. Try to introduce more nutritional dishes gradually. Choose a day of the week when you can 'experiment', but above all, try to make it fun. Try to engage their imaginations, you never know, as kids often seem to do, they could probably teach you a thing or two in the process.

That's the good news; the bad news is you cannot escape from the facts. Natural foods are better for you than processed foods. Whole foods, as their name implies, are complete, mass produced foods invariably are not. And, you might not want to hear this, fresh fruit and vegetables are the best way of transferring the energy of the sun direct into our bodies, there's no other way of putting it except to say that you can never eat too well, you can only eat too much.

1.24 Colloidal Minerals and Vitamins

A few years ago I came across the phenomenon of Colloidal Minerals and Vitamins. Colloidal minerals and vitamins are purely plant based and differ from other minerals and vitamins which are primarily metallic based, here's how it works. Minerals and vitamins are found in the soil in metallic form, we grow the plants which absorb the nutrients from the ground and store them in colloidal form in the food we eat. We absorb colloidal minerals and vitamins far better than metallic minerals and vitamins. This is because colloidal minerals and vitamins can be absorbed directly through our cell membranes, whereas metallic minerals and vitamins are only absorbed through the stomach and even then only in proportions of around four to six percent! (And lessening with age) This is part of our basic life chemistry. Plants absorb metallic minerals, which in turn are absorbed by organic species, which return to the earth to provide nutrition to the soil.

There is an old argument which says that if you eat enough fruit and vegetables then there is no need to take any supplement, however, recent evidence has shown that the foods we eat are slowly but surely being depleted of their mineral and vitamin content through over intensive agricultural farming methods. This is the main reason behind the increase in organic produce. To me it makes perfect sense. If a field only has 'x' amount of nutrients and we, year in and year out, use this field to produce say potatoes, then after a given period of time the soil will have fewer nutrients, if any at all, and therefore the potatoes themselves will consequently contain less nutrition. Farmers are also aware of this hence the growth in the use of fertilisers. Organic farming methods use no artificial fertilisers but with the concerns due to E-Coli and other harmful bacteria, even the use of organic fertilisers has been a cause for concern. So, how do we strike a balance? We must take colloidal minerals and vitamins as a regular supplement in order for us to have complete and chemical free nutrition.

Colloidal minerals and vitamins primarily come from one vast source in the state of Utah in the USA where, during the Jurassic Period a huge forest existed. This forest, over geological time, was covered by a comparatively thin layer of rock which, instead of being compressed down to form fossil fuels such as coal or oil, remained in vegetable form (a bit like peat moss) and created a nutritionally rich cocktail of over seventy-seven colloidal minerals and vitamins. It is like nature's storeroom and is a unique source of these precious supplements. Experts would argue that these supplements could actually prolong life span as well as allowing one to function fully.

This in turn gives us greater mental as well as physical stability. Take, for instance, selenium which has long been associated with mental health and routinely prescribed to mental health sufferers. Selenium in colloidal form is more easily absorbed and with very little treatment the sufferer is able to maintain their mental stability and self-control. Also Mercury when it is in metallic form it is poisonous but in colloidal form is extremely beneficial. Metallic silver is certainly nice to wear, but in colloidal form is an effective pro-biotic and although metallic copper has a multitude of uses in colloidal form can actually prevent ones hair turning grey!

1.25 Cooking

This may, upon first consideration, sound like a case of stating the obvious but another important factor in dictating the quality of our diet is not just what we cook but how we actually cook it. The process of cooking is not merely a mundane chore that we have to perform in order to eat, although most of us choose to see it that way. No, it's far more important than that. It is a way for us to engage our other centres, particularly the emotional, and really explore 'the art of cooking'. If you wish to convince yourself that cooking is tiresome, you can. All you need to do is programme yourself whilst you are cooking to have an inner dialogue that goes something like this. 'This is a pain in the arse', or 'I can't be bothered doing this', and the more you do that the more you will hate cooking! But if you learn to enjoy it and guess what, you really will, it really is as simple as that. There are also other benefits in that your food seems to taste better too.

Try this next time you are cooking; do it deliberately, don't just do it in autopilot. First of all observe what you are doing and the way you are doing it. The way you use knives, The very individual way you peel and slice vegetables, notice the way it's only you that does it that way (try watching someone else chopping to confirm this) and realise that it's something you do well.

Also try and engage all of your senses, because that is the beauty of cooking, it combines all five senses, so use them! You see, say a carrot, and you can tell, even before you touch it, from it's colour if it is fresh or not, if it is shiny or shrivelled. Next you confirm this when you pick up the carrot. You squeeze it to see if it soft or firm then, as you peel it, you can smell it, and of course when you cut it you can taste it. Lastly have you ever listened to what a fresh carrot sounds like when you crunch away at it? Or the sound of the first bite of an apple? Great isn't it? By engaging all your senses you tap directly into your emotional centre and a sense of real enjoyment and appreciation can come from it. Incidentally this is where the tradition of clinking glasses together stems from as it engages all five senses. First of all we look at the wine, we then smell it, when we taste it we also engage our sense of touch and the only one missing is our sense of sound so we clink glasses to engage this!

There are some that take this concept a little further and worship the food that they take as if it were a sacred offering. Many people still say 'Grace' before food as if it were a divine gift, giving thanks for the food laid before them. There is even a Buddhist meditation simply called 'eating meditation' where the participant concentrates on every sight, texture, smell, flavour and sound of their eating experience. Now, I'm not suggesting that we should all go off in some sort of trance next time we sit down to tuck into your beans on toast, everything in moderation but try it every now and then and you will find that cooking becomes a lot more pleasurable.

However there can often be a problem engaging our emotions when we cook in that they can be the wrong ones! I urge you to never cook when you are upset or angry; because that is all you will be serving when you eat. The fact of the matter is you get to eat your own emotions or worse still, serve them up to someone else! You are quite literally spitting venom into your food. As food tastes nicer when you enjoy cooking it, it follows that food tastes worse when negative emotions are added to the mix. This is because as all food contains living energy, call it Chi if you like, and as you prepare the food your own Chi combines with that of the food (it certainly does as you digest it). Then if you are angry when you are cooking then that negative anger energy will cancel out any good that the food is doing in the first place. I have often refused a dish that has been prepared by someone in a negative emotional state as I believe that I would almost be polluting myself with someone else's effluent!

On a more positive note the reverse is also true. Let's use an example of cooking a nice romantic meal for your partner; you certainly wouldn't want to do it if you were in a really foul mood with them. No, it's normally because you want to do it out of love and appreciation, or even a celebration like an anniversary, and just as you prepare and serve it with love then that is what you, and your partner are eating, your love and appreciation. Now, how much more satisfying is that? In this case the positive Chi that you have prepared the food with is like a marinade, it soaks into the meal, and it oozes goodness. However, this type of cooking should not be limited to when you are only cooking for others; it should also apply when you are cooking for yourself. It is like showing yourself respect. When you enjoy cooking for yourself you are saying to yourself that 'only the best will do', why? Because you are the best! Think about it this way, if your Guru came to your house to dine, would you not show them the utmost courtesy? Would you not pull out all the stops? Of course you would, so why not for Guru-U?

1.26 Variety (inc. food groups)

We have all heard the saying that 'variety is the spice of life', so imagine what our lives would be like if we did not have a varied diet. Historical records tell us that before the great Irish potato blight of the nineteenth century, the average Irishman ate between eight and ten pounds of potatoes per day, every day! In fact in vast areas of the world (particularly southeast Asia) many millions of people still rely on single food sources (in this case rice) as the main staple part of their diet. I don't know about you but I find it incredible that these people don't die of boredom, let alone malnutrition. Each food not only gives us a different nutritional benefit but also gives us a far greater sensory experience when eating.

As a reminder, here are the basic food groups:

Carbohydrates: Breads, Pastas, Rice etc.

Proteins: Meats and fish.

Fats: Dairy products.

Starches: Root vegetables.

Sugars: Soft fruits and vegetables.

Again, much has been written regarding the importance of each and every food group and there is a whole plethora of information widely available for further study. All I will add here is that each of the food groups in themselves are important energy sources depending on the type of activity we are involved in e.g. during moderate or high intensity aerobic exercise most of our energy comes from carbohydrates. Whereas during low intensity exercise both fats and carbohydrates, provide most of our energy. Proteins only seem to be used up after long periods of heavy exercise, for example running a marathon.

More recently diets such as The Atkins 'Diet' state that by completely removing one of these food groups, in this case carbohydrates, we will somehow 'fool' our bodies into burning more fat. I and many others like me say this, all of the food groups exist for particular and special reasons and to deprive our bodies of any of the essential food sources is to dabble in things that could well have long-term detrimental effects on your body. I suggest erring on the side of caution if you are considering embarking on this course of drastic action. A more sensible course of action may well be to consider what is known as 'food combining' where intensive studies in this field have shown that certain foods are best ate with others and some foods are best when not combined with others. For example, the combination of fats and carbohydrates when eaten together (e.g. pizza) has been shown to be difficult to digest. Also fruits should be eaten at the beginning of the meal rather than at the end (as in fruit salad).

Remember that variety is important and that if we deprive ourselves of any of the food groups, either though deliberate action (diet) or by neglect ('I don't like sprouts' etc.) then we are tampering with the sophisticated mechanism of our bodies that has taken thousands of years of evolution to perfect. It is important to maintain variety in all things and food is no exception.

1.27 Choose your own weight

One of the greatest fallacies of our time is that we are all supposed to be an 'ideal' weight. There are even machines nowadays where you can weigh yourself, input you height and body build (small, medium or large) and it can tell you not only what your weight is but what your 'ideal' weight should be (known as Body Mass Index - BMI.) Recently I tried out one of these and was told that I'm supposedly over 3 stone overweight! At the time I knew that I was carrying some extra weight, hence the reason to weigh myself in the first place, but I did not consider myself that much overweight and I knew that if I were to lose over 3 stone I would be nothing but skin and bone. What I say is this, take no notice of what the machine, or table or diagram says (accepting of course if it says that you are obese) is your ideal weight, and you choose your ideal weight.

Most of us know if we need to do something about our weight, or more precisely, how much fat we are carrying and the state of our muscle tone and some of us are fortunate enough to be able to do something about it relatively quickly. For instance I know that I need to lose around 1 stone (not 3!) to be what I would consider as my ideal weight or, more importantly, the weight that I feel happy with which is, after all, the only weight you *ought* to be, not what anybody else says you *should* be.

Unfortunately there are a great many people who are not as fortunate as I am with being able to lose weight when I want as there are countless individuals who constantly seem to be on some form of diet or other. Usually you will find that most of the people read 'pulp magazines' and are always measuring themselves up against the 'celebrity body beautiful' and, surprise surprise, they can never match up no matter how hard they try. So what they end up doing is disappointing themselves and then becoming disillusioned with their diet and move on to the next fad or craze or gadget (or celebrity wonder diet) that promises to create the body beautiful. I often wonder how many cycling and rowing machines that have been used a few times and then banished to the garage or the spare room never to be used again (but certainly never thrown out because that would be like admitting defeat) litter houses around the country.

Let me clear this up once and for all, unless you have got a personal trainer who works out with you 4-5 times per week then you are never going to measure up to the celebrity body beautiful. Most people who are in the business of looking good, pop stars, actors and models, look so because that is their job. Think of footballers and athletes, why is it, do you think, that they look so good? It's because they work damn hard to get that way. It takes years of dedication, it doesn't happen overnight. And unless you have got that amount of time (and money) to dedicate to honing your body to that extent you are never going to come close to their physique, it just won't happen, so dispel this thinking right now and stop disappointing yourself. Be content with the fact that you are a busy person in a busy world with a busy life and then find time in between to be able to work on your body as much as you can. And learn to be content with the shape and size that you are. There's no point in worrying if you are say as size 12 but you want to be a size 8, all you are going to do is be continually disappointed in yourself and lead a miserable life by saying to yourself some of the worst self slanders that you can like, 'I'm too fat' or (worst of all) 'I'm ugly'. Let's put it another way, if you want respect from others then the first thing you are going to have to do is respect yourself. If you want encouragement from others you have to encourage yourself first, and if you want praise from others about how well you look, then, guess what, you are going to have to learn to praise yourself first.

Now, by self-praise I don't mean to go home and find a few photographs of ourselves and create an altar and burn candles and incense, not at all. What I mean is what we say about ourselves and to ourselves in our inner dialogue which dictates not only the way we see ourselves, and of course the way others see us, but also the way we actually function. For instance, if all we ever say to ourselves is 'God, I'm tired' guess how you are going to feel? If all we ever say to ourselves is 'I'll never amount to anything in life', then guess what, you probably won't. The industrialist Henry Ford famously once stated *'Whether you think you can, or think you can't, you're probably right'*. Time and time again it has been proven that we all live up (or down) to our own expectations. So if all we ever say to ourselves is that we are fat or ugly then not matter how much weight we lose, no matter what size we go down to in our clothes, it will never be good enough because we have programmed ourselves to always feel bad about ourselves.

Ok, it's good to have a target. For instance if you are going on holiday or to a special occasion like a wedding and you want to be able to buy some new clothes that are a size too small for you, it will do your self esteem a whole lot of good when you can fit into those clothes and look and feel fabulous, however, how long does that feeling last? It always passes doesn't it? And, let's face it, if you are naturally a certain size then why not be comfortable with the size that you are, and comfortable in the knowledge that with a little effort you can become your ideal weight at any time. That's what I mean about finding your own weight because this way you need never be disappointed about your weight and shape again. In fact this ultimately leads to being proud of who you are, the way you are and the only expectations you have about yourself are your own, and nobody else's.

Once more I would like to add a word of caution here. Don't allow this to be an excuse to be lazy. I would hope that the standards you set yourself are both high, as well as realistic and achievable. And remember that you are never going to be as young as you are right now so make the most of it by accepting the fact that the exercise and diet that you can now accommodate will not be the same in 10 or 20 years time (all the more reason to do as much as you can right now!) Don't be slack, but don't be too hard on yourself either. Just go for it!

1.28 Macrobiotics

Macrobiotics is the science of maintaining a balanced diet as a way to maintain and improve one's health by restoring balance and harmony within ourselves, the food that we eat and our environments without having to rely on medicine or clinical treatments. Macrobiotics states that we can take control of our own health by returning to using simple, traditional and seasonal foods which can balance out our 'Yin' and 'Yang' energies (the basis of Chi.) This in turn balances our physical energies giving us a whole plethora of benefits.

The term macrobiotics was first used by the Japanese teacher and writer George Ohsawa in the 1940's and derives from the Greek words 'macro' (meaning 'big') and 'bios' (meaning 'life') i.e. big life, or more precisely, how to make our lives bigger and fuller.

The benefits of a macrobiotic lifestyle include:

- Greater energy, stamina and zest for life.
- Better memory function and learning ability
- Sharper awareness and alertness
- Improved emotional stability
- Physical flexibility and heightened sensitivity
- More open to spirituality and intuition
- Stronger immune system and greater recovery from illness and injury
- Improved outlook on life and behaviour

As we have discovered perfect balance comes in threes. The three important aspects to achieving balance through macrobiotics are:

1. Our diet. As human beings we have evolved over thousands of years and our modern diet is not always compatible.

2. Our Lifestyle. Our ancestors rarely stayed up late into the dark hours so we must try to sleep and rise earlier and to exercise more regularly.

3. Our Spirituality. We must try to awaken our dormant sense of spirit and to acknowledge our own responsibility to ourselves. Once we truly accept that we are indeed in control of our own health and well being we are a step closer to understanding that we are our own Guru's and spiritual advisers.

We will go into more detail about the concept and meaning of Yin and Yang in other chapters but for now we will define it as the opposite and complementary energies that exist within the universe (light and dark, north and south, winter and summer etc). In terms of macrobiotics Yin and Yang also applies to the foods that we eat as well as the seasons in which they grow in and the way that they are cooked as well as how they impact on our constitution. For example if we are for example tired, cold and slow then we are considered as being Yin in nature. But if we are hot in nature (aggressive, stubborn, angry etc) then we are considered to be more Yang. What macrobiotics aims to do is balance our constitution by preparing and eating foods that are opposite to us. So if we are too Yang then we must eat more Yin foods and vice versa. There is no point eating hot and spicy foods if we are looking to cool ourselves down. It would obviously be better if we were to eat more cooling or relaxing foods such as fruit, ice cream and cold drinks (fortunately including quite a wide variety of alcoholic beverages!)

Similarly if we were to live in an excessively hot climate then it is far more sensible to eat foods that will cool us down rather than heat us up, would it not? Conversely if we are working outdoors in the middle of winter then the last things we will have in mind for something to eat would be a nice salad followed by ice cream. When our environmental conditions are extremely Yin then we tend to eat more Yang foods which are hotter.

I am not able to give this vast and fascinating subject its due consideration in such a small subsection (my advice is for you to study more on the subject should you wish to do so). However, here are a few generalities as to what foods are considered as being either Yin or Yang.

Yang foods tend to grow in colder climates. They grow slowly and tend to be smaller, shorter, harder and drier normally growing below the ground. Yin foods tend to prefer warmer climates and grow faster, larger and taller. They also tend to be softer, more watery and tend to grow above the ground.

The way the food is prepared also has a dramatic effect on whether it is considered either Yin or Yang. In fact one can take the same food and depending on the way it is prepared can change it from one to the other. For example, take the humble tomato which is considered as a cooling Yin food. However if we take lots of tomatoes and make a soup (by applying lots of heat) or add the tomatoes to say, a curry then these would be considered as much more Yang.

The basics for cooking are the same the world over and depend upon four main factors;

- **Fire** - the application of heat
- **Time** - how long it is cooked for
- **Pressure** - if we use a lid or an oven
- **Salt** - how much we add to the food, (including most spices).

Generally, the more we use these fours factors the more Yang the food becomes and the less we use them, the more Yin. Raw food is generally more Yin (salads and raw vegetables) but food that requires a lot of heat to prepare (soups and stews) the outcome will be more Yang. Therefore it is very important to balance both the foods we eat as well as the way they are prepared.

Ranging from Yin at the top to Yang at the bottom here is the list of basic cooking techniques to refer to;

- Raw
- Blanching
- Boiling
- Steaming
- Sauté
- Pickling
- Stir-frying
- Pressure cooking
- Baking
- Deep-frying

Finally, before we can determine the kinds of food that we should or should not be eating we must first diagnose our current condition to determine whether or not we are either too Yin or too Yang. In order to do this accurately I suggest that you either seek a professional opinion from a recognised macrobiotic practitioner or by studying the subject in greater detail yourself as there is now a mass of information available on this rich and varied subject to answer even the most detailed enquiries.

In closing this section on diet I wish you the best of luck in finding your complete balanced and varied diet. It is a quest that can take many years but it is a challenge well worth completing for the years of rewards that it can offer in terms of health and wellbeing and as with most things, if it's worth anything at all it's worth working at.

PREVENTION

The world of preventative medicine, although certainly the oldest form of medicine known to man, is only recently being appreciated in the West and finally being given the recognition that it deserves. This ignorance of the benefits of preventative medicine is partially due to the influence of the powerful drug companies maintaining their insidious self-interests in supplying drugs that tend to mask the symptoms of illness rather than attempting to provide a cure as well as their obvious reluctance to research and develop alternative therapies.

It is well recognised that our body's own healing mechanisms and immune system has the potential to be more powerful than any drug known to the pharmaceutical industry. It is such a wonder to modern medicine that scientists still do not fully understand even its most basic mechanisms. Surely this should be the future of medical research where the body itself is its own portable drug manufacturing plant? Unfortunately as these types of therapies are very difficult, if not impossible, to patent they are therefore not considered as financially viable. In fact the pharmaceutical companies would rapidly go out of business if, within each of us, we were able to produce the chemicals that they sell us, so it's obvious that they won't be spending much time or effort on something as self defeating. What we must do as individuals is to try to break the cycle of illness-drugs-illness and attempt to find our own solutions rather than waiting for somebody else to take that responsibility.

Some people still find the idea of complementary and alternative therapies as somehow being restricted to 'Mother Earth Types' or 'tree-hugging' New Age Vegans. And, even though countless benefits have been researched and documented, the vast majority of people still consider them as being some kind of quack therapies. We have certainly come a long way from the proverbial 'Snake Oil' and moved a whole lot closer to a truer understanding of Holistic Medicine which looks at the body as a whole mechanism rather than merely a collection of individual parts. As modern science expands our awareness of the wonder of the human body and all its complexities it is coming closer to understanding what has been known for countless generations. Some so-called alternative therapies have been extremely beneficial in the healing of sickness for hundreds, if not thousands, of years and as science still demands empirical proof to say conclusively if the theory is confirmed in practice, then the testimonies of those countless numbers who have benefitted from alternative therapies speaks volumes. (But don't wait for the drug companies to advertise these facts or you will be waiting for a very long time!)

We have all heard the saying 'prevention is better than the cure' but what does it mean? It's like the old saying 'a stitch in time saves nine' where if we do a little work beforehand we save ourselves a whole lot of work at a later date as the crux of the problem is the sad fact that once our health deteriorates, it's normally too late to do much about it. Wouldn't it be better if we could avoid illness in the first place rather than treat it when it occurs? That's what preventative medicine is all about.

Again, consider your Guru as the one you revere, the one who you would do anything for, as the one you want to spend as much time as you possibly can with. Now consider this, how would you feel if they died before their time? Devastated probably? Now consider yourself. How would your family and friends and the ones who love and cherish you feel if you were to die before your time? (I hope the answer is the same as above.) Therefore you owe it to them, as well as to yourself, to be as healthy as you can for as long as you can so that you can live a full life for them and for you and to live this way for as long as possible.

So how do you do this? Simple, and as with most other things, by taking complete responsibility for yourself (again, nobody else is going to do it for you) and to make a lifelong determination to take your health seriously for, as the old saying goes, 'you will either use it or lose it.' The stakes are that high but fortunately, the steps to reach health and vitality are not, they are simple and easy and once you become aware of how they are realised you will not want to live without them.

1.31 The importance of exercise

This may seem at first glance to be reiterating what we have already discussed about exercise when we were exploring exercise in the context of balancing our physical aspect. This section however is more concerned with the offshoot benefits that exercise can bring to preventing illness from occurring in the first place in terms of the benefits that exercise can have on our immune system. Time and again it has been proven that the fitter you are the more able you are to deal with everyday illnesses such as the common cold or in reducing recovery periods after surgical procedures and operations. In short fitter people are much less likely to be ill and tend to heal a lot quicker than their unfit counterparts. Regular exercise kicks in our own in-built chemical processing plant (our immune system) which produces good medicine whilst at the same time ridding our body of the bad chemicals that in some cases are the actual root causes of sickness (e.g. free radicals.)

The other day whilst I was out riding my mountain bike up a rather steep hill I was just at the point when it was really beginning to hurt and I was starting to consider getting off and pushing when I thought to myself that if my life depended on getting to the top of the hill very quickly, I could do it. I'd find the energy from somewhere if, say my life, or the lives of my loved ones, were at stake. The adrenalin would serge through me and I'd be at the top and over the other side in an instant, so why couldn't I summon up that energy when I needed it? Then it came to me in a flash! My life does depend on it or at least the quality of my life and is that not what we are discussing here, not just life, but our quality of life? I know that if I don't exercise the quality of my life reduces, and when I do it increases. But also if the quality of my exercise is poor, then the quality of my life is also poor. You only get out what you put in and as we discussed earlier with exercise and energy, the more you burn up, the more you get back in return. Or if you prefer the more scientific approach; energy cannot be created or destroyed, it merely changes from one form to another.

However, there are even greater benefits to the body's immune system through sustained physical exercise as it has been proven that it significantly reduces stress. Later we will discuss in greater detail the impact stress has on our immune system but at this moment it is worth stating that stress is known to be a major contributing factor in determining how well our bodies can fend off and cope with sickness. Bottom line, the more stressed we are, the worse our immune system functions and the higher the possibility of us becoming ill. Therefore we truly do hold in our own hands the potential to keep ourselves healthy and, if necessary, to cure ourselves should we succumb to illness. After all, is that not the best place that a cure should be? Drug companies are primarily motivated by profit and although it is considered as a highly noble profession to be in the venture to cure the likes of cancer, unfortunately it is not solely motivated by humanitarianism, perversely it is because a whole lot of money would also be made along the way. No, it's us that holds that key in our hands. We can make the choices for the sake of our own health and not leave it in the hands of doctors who are a bit like mechanics; they can only fix it if it's broken. Go and see a doctor when you're perfectly healthy and they'll say there's nothing they can do for you. But the painful truth is that sometimes the reverse is also true. When you go to see your doctor when you are sick, he may still tell you there is nothing he can do for you 'except to make you comfortable' and when we hear that infamous saying we know it's never good news.

1.32 Stress Management

"Every instant of time is a pinprick of eternity. All things are petty, easily changed, vanishing away." Marcus Aurelius.

Okay, so we except that stress can make us ill, but what can we actually do about it? First of all we have to understand what we define as stressful before we can try to deal with its effects. So what do we mean when we talk about stress or being 'stressed out'? The dictionary definition of stress is as follows; *constraining or impelling force; physical, mental or emotional strain; tension, pressure, violence; weight, importance, or influence; force exerted upon or between the parts of the body.* Therefore when we are stressed a force is acting upon us which causes both physical and emotional strain on our bodies to the point of actual violence! So where does this force come from that can do this much harm? Look around, the world can be a very stressful place. Our jobs may be in danger and we may be facing an uncertain future, this will make us stressed. Conversely our jobs could be that certain and boring that we feel trapped, this will lead to an inevitable feeling of discomfort with resultant stress. Even driving to work and sitting in traffic jams, or even trying to find a parking space can stress us out. Our jobs themselves may well be stressful, especially if we don't get on with our co-workers and employers. Tests have proven that if you cage any animal they will suffer from stress and that they are more likely to die earlier as their immune systems become impaired. Tests have also shown that our heart rate increases when we are stuck in traffic, which results in our fight or flight reflex being employed at a completely inappropriate time. This primordial reflex was meant to get us out of a dangerous situation but now unfortunately it tends to put us into one!

Where else does stress manifest itself? In virtually every single aspect of our lives, that's where. If our family relationships are strained we experience stress. When we watch the news we experience stress, when our favourite team loses a game we feel stress. There are countless other ways that stress can exert its insidious force upon us and it's true that given the same situations some people seem to deal with the resultant stresses and strains better than others. Some people are downed by it while others seem to be uplifted. The inevitable fact is that we all experience some form of stress to a greater or lesser degree at some time in our lives. It could also be said that a life without stress is not a life at all; it's another ad-man's dream that simply doesn't exist in the real world. So how is it that some deal with it better than others? Why is it some people seem better equipped to deal with stress? Is it because some people have had more experience in dealing with stress and have become used to employing strategies that enable them to cope? Possibly, but I think that the answer lies within and our attitude when it comes to dealing with stressful situations.

There are some people who have such a dreadful fear of anything stressful that they try to avoid it like the plague which is a bit like trying to avoid getting wet in the shower and when stress hits them they simply can't cope. This unhealthy aversion can often lead these people to living a more stressful life in the first place. The secret, I believe, lies in our attitude. If we have the kind of attitude that knows that there will be times in our lives when we seem stretched to the very limit and accept these times that are 'sent to test us' (and not just in a resigned way but in a proactive way), then we will certainly deal with them a lot better when those stressful situations inevitably appear. What I am not saying is that we should always be waiting for our next stressful event to happen to us in order to prove our resilience, as this would probably stress us out more than ever, but what I am saying is that when it does happen we must possess the resolve to weather the storm. We must fortify ourselves with the attitude of 'no matter what'. Change your inner dialogue from 'I can't cope' to 'I will cope, no matter what'. This will inevitably result in being able to deal with whatever life may, and probably will, throw our way.

We must also cultivate the attitude of being able to 'turn poison into medicine'. This means that no matter what challenges we are facing we must try to find a way of turning the circumstances around to our advantage. Dr. Hatsumi used to say *"If you have to fight then you will obviously do your best to avoid being struck. However, you must accept the fact that you will inevitably be struck, but what you must do is to try to find a way to use this power against your opponent."* In other words, the stronger the challenges the more opportunity we have to develop, as in the saying:

> *"Adversity gives birth to greatness. The greater the challenges and difficulties we face, the greater the opportunity we have to develop and grow as people, A life without adversity, a life of ease and comfort, produces nothing and leaves us with nothing. This is one of the indisputable facts of life."* Daisaku Ikeda.

1.33 Acupuncture

Take acupuncture, for example. Millions, possibly even billions, of people throughout the world can testify to the therapeutic value of this form of alternative therapy. To me it is simply more than alternative; it is in fact my primary source of treatment for my long-term back pain condition. For many years, since sustaining an injury whilst practising an inappropriate form of Martial Art for my stature and age at the time, I have used acupuncture as an effective and drug-free treatment to my often painful and debilitating condition.

Once again I will only be able to scrape the surface of this most wonderful subject in the space we have available in the hope that this generates enough interest for you to want to research it further. Acupuncture has been used for over three thousand years and states that our bodies are alive because of 'electrical impulses' within our bodies, known as Chi, which flows around our bodies through a system known as 'Meridians'. These meridians, or pathways, are occasionally blocked and the energy can no longer flow correctly resulting in pain and if these pathways are ignored and left untreated the resultant conditions can even become life threatening. For instance if our organs, such as our heart and lungs, are not working to full capacity how can we be expected to be 'firing on all cylinders'? The answer is we can't. And if our condition is not diagnosed and treated accordingly our heart and lungs will eventually cease to function altogether resulting, inevitably, in disease and death. Obviously this is not limited just to the function of our heart and lungs but also all of our other organs and our overall immune system.

Although acupuncture can be used to treat an existing illness or condition it is primarily a form of preventative medicine in that it believes it is far better to stop illness happening before it starts rather than cure it after it has occurred. It is also, in the case of damage already occurring, an excellent form of complementary medicine in that it can work very well in combination with many other forms of treatment. For instance, many people who undergo drastic treatment for their cancers, such as radiation therapy and chemotherapy find that the resultant sickness and nausea can be equally, if not more so, debilitating than the actual illness itself. So much so that many people often refuse further treatment and allow 'nature to run its course'. In some cases regular acupuncture has been proved to alleviate a lot of these common side effects allowing cancer sufferers, not only the chance of leading a relatively normal life, but also the often life-saving commencement of further treatment.

My own personal experience of acupuncture is when I have used it to treat a specific condition (that being for pain relief due to a trapped nerve in my spine) I found that it worked extremely well. There were occasions when I was unable to walk unaided into the treatment centre and then to be able to 'bound' out afterwards. However I did have to revert to surgery in order to rectify the problem with my back but continually used acupuncture as a way of boosting my immune system and thereby increasing my chances of a full and speedy recovery. Fortunately this has been the case and although I now enjoy a healthy and active life I still use acupuncture as a way of keeping my Chi in balance.

I also employed acupuncture to overcome a case of Bells Palsy. I woke up one morning and the whole of the left side of my face was paralysed, it drooped as if I'd actually suffered a stroke. I was told by the doctors that I would just have to 'wait and see' to see if my condition improved and that in most cases it would take between 3-4 months, but in some cases the paralysis would remain, so it was straight down to the acupuncturist for me and with a course of half a dozen treatments over a two week period it had completely disappeared – what a relief as well as further proof to myself that this was far more than circumstantial evidence of its efficacy.

Another fascinating fact about acupuncture is that it can have beneficial effects even when there is no specific condition to treat. A good acupuncturist will recommend at least four treatments per year as a way of maintaining balance. This occurs when there is a change in the Earth Chi at the beginning and end of each season, as Summer Chi is different to Winter Chi. In the summer our Chi is very Yang or rising and in the winter our Chi is very Yin or lowered. In the spring and autumn it is moving from one form to the other.

So, as we tune our bodies into the natural cycles of nature we are less likely to suffer illness. A good example of this is our propensity to get some kind of cold or flu after we have returned from a winter sun holiday. Due to the nature of my work I found it much more convenient to holiday over the Christmas and New Year period and would often fly to sunnier climes. However, on returning I would find, more often than not, that within a short period of returning home I would end up with some bad cold, flu, and in one year an extremely painful case of chicken pox. When I mentioned this to my acupuncturist he explained to me why. During the darkest depths of winter our Yin energy is highest and our Yang energy is more subdued. However, as soon as we get out into the bright sunshine our Yang energy goes 'whoopee' and takes over, giving us a burst of summer energy. Then, two weeks later when we get back home to a dark winter, our Yang energy doesn't know what is happening and asks 'Well is it summer of not'? This results in the natural flow of our Yin and Yang energies being disrupted and therefore confusing the immune system resulting in inevitable illness. I mean, let's face it, international travel for all is only a thing of the last century and our bodies simply don't adapt to those kind of environmental changes that quickly, evolution unfortunately takes much longer. So, from that moment on I haven't taken winter break holidays in the sun and haven't experienced that kind of imbalance since.

So, what if the thought of having needles pushed into the skin is not your idea of pleasure? Well, first of all you can overcome your irrational fear and realise that the therapeutic benefits of acupuncture far outweighs your fear of needles, or simply to consider another way to stimulate your meridians and your Chi. One of the ways of doing this is through 'acupressure'. This is in essence acupuncture but without the needles and can produce the same benefits. Unfortunately acupressure practitioners are very difficult to find and because they are such a rarity they tend to charge their fees accordingly. Another way to experience the benefits of acupuncture without the use of needles is through what are known as section cups where these are applied to our skin over the acupuncture point and literally suck the negative, or what is termed our 'sickness Chi' out of our bodies. What I would suggest is that you shop around. Try talking to an acupuncturist and talk to them about your fears, who knows they might even have a treatment for overcoming the fear of needles!

1.34 Massage

If stress is one of the major causes of disease in the modern world then what else can we do to relieve that stress? Have you ever had a really good massage where you come away feeling light as a cloud and ready to take on whatever the rest of the day has got to throw at you? And, if not, why not? Remember your Guru is like your very own personal trainer and they would certainly recommend that you take this form of treatment as often as you possibly can.

Massage is one of the oldest and most basic forms of remedial and complementary therapies and dates back to before Egyptian times. Archaeological evidence has discovered all manner of artefacts relating to the extensive use of massage in ancient Egypt such as jars of aromatic oils as well as implements such as combs and spoons that were used to apply oils and to remove dead skin. The Greeks and the Romans too used massage extensively as a way of improving the body's recovery after exercise. How many times have you seen on television a physiotherapist rubbing the legs of an athlete after a run, ride, swim or football match? Why do they do this? And how is massage so effective?

The word massage is thought to have come from either the Greek word meaning knead or from the Arabic meaning press softly. In 1000BC the great writer Homer mentioned in his Odyssey women 'rubbing and anointing war torn heroes' to refresh them after battle. Even ancient civilisations believed in the importance of exercise, bathing and massage in order to look and feel better. Our whole concept of the 'body beautiful' stems from this time when it was only the rich that could afford the time to spend developing their physique (much as it seems today).

Later, at around 500BC, the Greek historian Herodotus began to apply exercise and massage in the treatment of disease and principles about how to rub and where to rub began to be formulated. Hippocrates, who many consider to be the founding father of medicine (indeed medical students must still take the Hippocratic Oath before they can become qualified doctors), also extensively used massage for treatment. He found that 'hard rubbing binds and soft rubbing loosens'. He also found benefits in improvements to the heart even though the circulatory system had not been discovered at the time.

So how does it actually work? When our muscles work they need a greater supply of oxygen, through increased blood supply, than when they are at rest and as they work they break the oxygen down and produce waste products, such as lactic acid, which can then accumulate in the muscles when resting thus resulting in stiffness. So, when the muscles are massaged the blood supply is increased and this feeds the muscles with more oxygen which has two direct effects; firstly the accumulated waste products are broken down to re-enter the bloodstream, and secondly the oxygen actually absorbs these toxic waste products leaving the muscles clean and refreshed.

Also, due to the effects of rubbing and friction heat is produced and consequently the whole body increases in temperature. That's why it's important to vigorously rub someone in the initial stages of hypothermia in order to increase their blood flow and to raise their core body temperature. Blood flows up to three times more quickly through a muscle which has been massaged and this increased blood supply also has the added benefit of increasing nutritional flow to the muscle fibre and in turn the whole of that muscle as well as the surrounding muscle group.

Massage also has a direct effect on the joints and bones as well as on our nerves. In the deeper layers of the epidermis lie the peripheral nerve endings which, when massaged, can become stimulated or soothed depending on the type of massage used. (Why do you think massage is so extensively used as a form of foreplay?) Direct contact with certain nerve endings can have a corresponding effect on specific parts of the body (hence the reason why acupuncture and acupressure work). Take for example the secretor nerves of the stomach, if they are stimulated through massage the stomach will produce more digestive juices to aid digestion and go a long way to alleviate digestive problems. The same is also true for all of the other organs in our bodies. When the nerves are stimulated through the application of pressure and rubbing then we experience beneficial effects. This is also true for the soothing effects of massage as we gain relaxation through slow rhythmic manipulations which can induce sleep by causing the nerve endings to produce natural sedatives.

I hope you have experienced the soothing and almost hypnotic effects of a good head, neck and shoulders massage and once again, if not, why not?

1.35 Aromatherapy

As previously mentioned the use of aromatic oils in massage has been widespread for thousands of years and more recently scientific studies have proven that certain plants contain substances which give specific health benefits. Yet this begs the questions how and why? Why do the essential oils of certain plants affect our biochemistry? Indeed what are essential oils anyway, and how do they affect us in different ways?

Aromatherapy is well recognised as a way of bringing balance into our lives as it aims to treat the whole person by taking into account their physical state as well as their emotional state as our emotions can have a dramatic and marked effect on our physical wellbeing. It works as a preventative medicine by strengthening our body's immune system so that we are better able to deal with illness and infection should it occur. As our senses are irrevocably linked so it goes without saying that should our sense of smell be affected, then all our other senses will be also. It has also been proven, even by conventional medicine, that certain plants contain medicinal benefits. (Most pharmaceutical drugs have initially been derived from plants. However, plants cannot be patented, whereas chemical synthetic bi-products can). Essential oils are the highly concentrated form of these plants and can be applied to the body through the skin (massage) or through our olfactory system (sense of smell).

The first evidence of the widespread use of essential oils comes from ancient Egypt in the form of perfumes, incense for religious use and for the process of embalming the dead prior to mummification. The Greeks and Romans acquired much of their knowledge from the Egyptians and used essential oils for massage and bathing purposes and discovered that certain aromatic plants were very relaxing while others were stimulating and commenced with the first classifications. Hippocrates wrote about a huge range of medicinal plants and stated that the best way to maintain good health was to have an aromatic bath and scented massage every day!

The earliest record of the use of essential oils in England was in the 13th century. With the invention and development of printing many books were produced confirming the benefits of certain herbs and plants. It is a well-known fact that during the plagues that ravaged Europe in the Middle Ages a large proportion of the ones who survived were those that used essential oils on a regular basis. This is due to the fact that certain essential oils have excellent antiseptic properties.

The modern scientific study of the medicinal benefits of essential oils is attributed to Rene Gattefosse, a 1920's cosmetics and perfume maker, and as with most great scientific breakthroughs came completely by accident. One day whilst making fragrances he managed to burn his arm quite badly and the only liquid close by was a vat of lavender oil. He quenched his arm in the cooling oil and later found that not only did he heal a lot quicker, but that the burn did not scar his skin. This discovery led him to undertake extensive research into the medicinal benefits of essential oils. His work revealed that essential oils can not only penetrate the layers of the skin but also that they can be carried by the circulatory system to various parts of the body including the lymphatic system, the immune system and to the organs themselves. However, during the middle part of the twentieth century herbal and aromatic therapies lost favour to the growth of modern pharmaceuticals and synthetic drugs. Fortunately the pendulum has now swung back completely in the direction towards the use of essential oils as people have become disillusioned with so called orthodox medicine.

Should you explore the possibilities of applying aromatherapy to maintaining your balance (which your Guru would certainly enjoy and therefore recommend that you do) then here are a few words of advice as to what to do and what to expect. Firstly make sure your initial consultation is with a fully qualified aromatherapist as the dangers of inappropriate treatment are very great indeed. The list of physical conditions where aromatherapy is not recommended is large and extensive (these are called contra-indications), ranging from high or low blood pressure to pregnancy. The problem nowadays is the common availability of essential oils in a huge variety of products ranging from shampoos and showers gels through to air fresheners. Also the use of oil burners has vastly increased in the last ten years and the profusion of relaxing or invigorating blends can seem quite confusing. Unfortunately there are some people who are doing themselves more harm than good by using these products inappropriately. My advice would be to either take professional advice or do your own research into what should be used and when and what should not.

A qualified aromatherapist will, through the process of consultation, give you a personal prescription as to what you should use and when and what you should avoid. The vast array of oils that are now available and their medicinal benefits can be more that a little confusing so it is always best to get the advice of a qualified practitioner before commencing any treatment. However when you do you may well find as many benefits as there are remedies ranging from increased energy levels, better sleep patterns, increased metabolism and a greater sense of physical and emotional wellbeing.

1.36 Relaxation

Relaxing may sound like the most common sense way of combating stress and when we think of relaxing we tend to think about what we do in our 'time off', what we do to unwind after work or how we spend our weekends and holidays. But there is a world of difference between relaxing and relaxation. Relaxing is a passive act whereas the art of relaxation requires effort and concentration (probably the reason why so many choose not to learn the art in the first place?) However, in order to learn the art of relaxation we must first learn how to relax.

Answer this question as honestly and with as much detail as possible (it may even help to write it down as a list to remind you.) *What is it that I do to relax and unwind?* Now give yourself 5-10 minutes to think. Your list can include anything and everything you consider as being relaxing, be it watching television, cooking and eating food, exercising, sleeping, drinking, having sex, walking, whatever you like.

Hopefully you now have a list and by the way, congratulations if you do! The problem in this mad hectic modern world is that some people don't even have a list and rack their brains for something to come up with. (Incidentally if you are this kind of person and you recognise that you need to invest more time in yourself and your leisure time then I recommend that you make an appointment with a qualified life coach who can help you establish a more healthy and balanced lifestyle). So, now that you have your list I now want you to think about how much time in an average week you actually spend doing these activities. (Once again spend a little time doing this and write down your findings).

Next I want you to try to quantify, using your own judgement, whether or not you consider those activities as being 'good' for you or 'bad' for you. For example it goes without saying that sleep is good for you, but too much sleep can often leave you feeling even more tired. Also if you eat or drink too much then you are often unable to do anything else. Allow Guru-U to 'talk' to you and allow yourself to listen. Now put a cross next to those things that fall into the category of 'too much of it is not always a good thing' and soon your list is not so long is it? This makes us realise that we all need to relax a lot more (and not just in our 'time off'!)

Once more the key is balance. We must observe ourselves in greater detail in order to understand what anger management consultants call 'the triggers' that make us feel agitated or irritable be it traffic, disagreements, obstacles or any other challenge that we face in our daily lives and to recognise the effects they are having on us. Because we can be sure that if we are left feeling unpleasant, stressed or ruffled in any way then we can bet that more cortisone, that you don't really need, has just come into your system. Once we have been made aware of this we soon begin to not only see but actually hear the triggers and to watch their effects, which are normally described as an agitated state, such as an increased heart and breathing rate, louder and quicker voice patterns, flushed and perspiring skin.

The naturally secreted hormone called cortisone is a little like adrenaline in that it occurs when we are agitated and that too greater an amount in our blood system leads to high blood pressure and other serious conditions. It is unlike adrenaline in that it is always there rather than simply released during fight or flight. When we sleep our cortisone levels are relatively low and as we wake they increase throughout the day, returning to a normal low level at night in order for us to sleep once more. However, abnormally high levels of cortisone late at night can and often do, result in sleeplessness and irritability. (Paradoxically irritability causes our cortisone levels to rise!)

When this happens I want you to imagine alarm bells ringing and lights flashing because this is not good for you! After a while you will know not only what the triggers are but also the events leading up to these episodes in the first place, and once you do this you can begin to control the outcomes. When you feel yourself 'rising' you can then make a conscious decision as to which way you now choose to react. Do you blow your top or keep your cool? It's entirely up to you because when all is said and done and no matter the provocation no one else can ever dictate to you your reaction, only you can. Yes, we all have emotional reactions to situations, that's what makes us human, but we have a choice as to whether or not we want to remain in that agitated state and for how long. Even if somebody swears at you or uses physical violence against you it is entirely up to you whether or not you perpetuate that aggression and guess what? When you decide to react in a different way the situation has a different outcome in exactly the inverse proportion than if you react in the same ways that you have always done you will always receive the same outcome!

Now that the first steps have been taken into learning how to reduce your cortisone levels you can now begin to look at other ways of *really* relaxing rather than *nearly* relaxing. It sounds so glib to say merely relax as it does require more effort than that. However, don't consider it as a chore that has to be completed, try to change your mindset into conditioning yourself that this is something that you can and must treat yourself to and, as with most things in life, when you really enjoy doing it you find yourself doing it more and more! Put some 'special time' aside for yourself. If you have family then talk to them and let them know what you are doing and the reasons why you are doing it. It's a bit like keeping to your diet or quitting smoking, it's best to ask for some support. Ask your family to give you the time and space that you need for yourself and try as much as you can to keep to that time diligently. If it is Sunday evening for instance then try to keep that time aside just for you and make it as much a part of your families schedule as it is yours.

Now, what are you going to do with this time to really relax? Again this is entirely up to you but here are a few tips and hints as to the basic requirements for learning true relaxation. As most of our energies in the West are 'rising' energies it is best if we try to 'lower' that energy as much as possible with the aid of either a nice relaxing bath, using relaxing essential oils such as lavender and the use of soft candle type lighting. Try to also use slow relaxing music to put you in a place of tranquillity where you can concentrate on your breathing and heart rate. (We will discuss slowing these down in the next section). You can then either completely relax in the water, although if it is either too hot or too cold then there is an obvious time limit for this. Try to bathe until you feel as though you are ready to dry off and relax some more. Again the method is down to your own suiting but always make sure you are most comfortable (usually lying down – but try not to fall asleep!) Make sure you are warm but not too hot, and then try to simply empty your mind of thoughts. Try not to think about what you have been doing or what you want to get done. Merely fall into yourself and switch off but only to the extent that you are still awake. Allow yourself to float between the waking and sleeping world until you feel refreshed, coming around in your own time. If you are just starting out then aim for 10-15 minutes and gradually increase this in time. (If this sounds a bit ambitious just try for 5-10 minutes at first). In this state your body is relaxed, your mind is at peace and your stress levels will invariably be lower and the more you do the lower they will become it's as simple as that. Congratulations! You now know how to relax!

1.37 Meditation

Now that you have learned the basics concerning true relaxation you can now begin to experience the immeasurable benefits of meditation. Before we begin to explore what meditation is and how it is beneficial in terms of preventative medicine, specifically to our physical being (more will be discussed in a later chapter on the benefits to our spiritual being), it is first worth describing what meditation is not. Meditation is not the proverbial 'transcendental' state (although it can be if you practice it enough) where you leave all of your earthly desires behind and everyday thoughts at the door and then enter a tranquil room bathed in light. Nor is it a place to escape to and play a version of grown-up hide and seek where you can lock yourself away from the world and pretend that it doesn't exist and that all your problems will simply vanish (ostrich's heads and sand come to mind!).

No, it is a far more dynamic thing than that! Meditation is a deliberate act that we uniquely perform as human beings and that no other being on this planet, or at least none that we know of, can do and that is to use our imaginations and to contemplate. (See Visualisation – section 3.26) We all possess this amazing ability to be able to sit and wonder, to coin a phrase 'to commune with the cosmos'. Human beings are the only species that through the very act of will alone can deliberately ask questions such as "Why am I here?" and "What is the meaning of my life and what is its purpose?" We can also ask ourselves what we can do in order to find and fulfil our purpose, what deliberate acts can we perform so we can shape our futures in order to leave our mark on the world?

Meditation has been described as a dialogue between the individual and the universe. It is a way for you to be able to tap into the energies of the vast universal life force that holds us and everything together. For once you start to believe that you are apart and somehow separate from this energy then you deny yourself an incredible opportunity.

Okay, so how do we actually go about performing meditation? First of all, like true relaxation, we must first allow ourselves the time and the space in order to get the very most out of it. There's no point in meditating in a room where others are watching TV or anywhere else that provides distractions. Meditation is not a team activity; it is a solitary journey to the centre of oneself and consequently can only be taken in isolation. True, there are meditation classes available to learn the basics where we can sit within a group whilst someone else teaches us the steps to take but when all is said and done it is only ourselves that can take those steps.

So, find yourself a place where you can sit comfortably. Seating is preferred to lying down as it minimizes the risk of falling asleep. It is best to sit with your spine completely straight be that by kneeling, with the aid of cushions if required, or on a straight backed chair. You can sit cross-legged if you are one of the supple few who can sit comfortably in this position for any length of time. However you decide to sit is completely up to you so long as the spine is straight as this improves energy flow. Once you are seated comfortably then you can begin to 'slow yourself down', this can be done with your eyes either open or closed, although closed is preferable in this particular instance. Concentrate on your breath, breathe in through your nose if you can, and out through your mouth. Then try and slow your breathing down by taking even deeper breaths. Yogic breathing comes from what is known as the 'base chakra' which is located at the lower tip of the spine. Imagine that your in breath comes directly from this point and as you inhale count to seven, hold your breath for one second and then exhale. While you are breathing imagine your energy rising from the base chakra right up through your spine to your head. This is to what is known as the 'third-eye chakra' which is located between the eyebrows and an inch higher. When you exhale again to a count of seven imagine a ball of energy travelling down through your body to your base chakra and then upon holding your breath for one second begin the cycle all over again by raising the ball of energy once more to your third-eye on the count of seven. (This is known as the 'earth cycle'.)

Repeat this cycle at least seven times until your breathing is long and deep. You can then let your breath become shallower and less regular. Breathe more naturally without counting and allow your mind to wander. When a thought enters your mind, honour that thought and like letting go of a balloon, let it go! Let go of all your thoughts and concerns and just allow yourself to be in the place that we human beings are meant to be, at peace and in harmony with the universe.

Now, try to radiate that sense of peace outwards by first imagining yourself surrounded by a warm glow just an inch or two from your skin. When this warm feeling is established try to expand the size of that ball of energy. What you will find is that over time this energy can extend as far as you want it to go! It becomes a positive life-force that can encompass and envelope not just the whole of your body but the very environment that you are in, where you live but also with whom you live, thus creating peace in your own life as well as the lives of all those around you. It is the most tremendous gift that you can give yourself and to those that you love. Peace and tranquillity. For what you will find is that this peace and tranquillity will move from beyond the confines of your meditation space (your room and your body) and manifest itself in your daily life. Previously those things that caused you angst will no longer have control over your actions and reactions. By transforming your inner reality you, in direct proportion, transform your outer reality, this is the power of meditation.

1.38 Chanting

All the matter in the universe is made up from atoms which all vibrate at a certain frequency which in turn dictates whether or not something is a gas, liquid or solid. The minute vibration of electrons and protons around a nucleus create the building blocks for all things including our bodies. Our bodies are neither separate or in any way apart from this universal energy but an integral and inseparable part.

Sound too is a vibration. The lower the frequency the 'deeper' the note and the higher the vibration the 'higher' the sound. When you create a sound you vibrate at a certain frequency depending on the sound you make, and those sounds have a direct impact on both your inner and outer environments. For instance, have you ever felt agitated when somebody is playing their personal stereo too loud or tranquil when you hear a pleasant piece of music? This is the impact that sounds on us; therefore it is true to say that the sounds that you produce impact elsewhere.

Recently I came across an article which stated that our very existence as the alpha species on the planet may well have resulted from our ability to vocalise. Specifically neurophysiologists have hypothesised that vocal vibrations associated with human language cause a kind of cleansing of what are known as the cerebrospinal fluids which are molecules in the spinal fluid which bathe and continuously purify the brain. These molecules are indeed a way of actually blowing out the cobwebs in our minds. It was also noted that as a species we are known to have a relatively thin skull structure this may well have had a positive adaptive advantage in terms of removing chemical waste products from our brains thus 'speeding up' its evolution when compared with other species with thicker skulls. In short, as we make a sound, it vibrates through our thin skulls, producing cleansing chemicals and thereby ensuring that our thought processes are clearer. Chanting is a very deliberate way of inducing this effect.

When I use the word chanting I'm sure a lot of you will have all kinds of prejudgements as to what this really means. Most of you will think of extreme religious practices with a hint of disapproval putting it down to either a lot of nonsense or mystical mumbo jumbo with no real connection to the modern world. However, as with most ancient practices, much is now known about the beneficial effects of creating certain sounds and repeating them over and over again in the form of a mantra. Most people are familiar with the sound of 'Om' or 'Aa' but the chant that I, and tens of millions of other people around the world use is the Buddhist chant of 'Nam Myoho Renge Kyo'. This is a chant that originates in medieval Japan as taught by the Buddhist scholar Nichiren Daishonin (1222-1282).

Nam Myoho Renge Kyo contains all of the sounds that are necessary to put us in harmony with the energy of the whole universe. I visualise it as being like a tuning fork that vibrates at the same frequency as the rest of the universe and by making this sound we too vibrate at the same frequency. When we do so we are in direct contact with that universal energy which we can then help us tap in to and use that energy to our benefit. Firstly, upon chanting it leaves one with a feeling not unlike meditation, of peace and tranquillity, but it is also a lot more than just a good feeling. For when we vibrate at the same frequency as the rest of the universe, the universe responds in a positive manner and we reap the rewards. The words 'harmony' and 'discord' come to mind. When we are in harmony with the universe the universe responds positively. When we are in discord with the universe the universe responds accordingly, normally with negative connotations. Buddhist philosophy says that it is not ourselves that is a reflection of our surroundings but it is we that create our environments around our life state.

Let me put it another way, conversely if we are constantly at odds with our environments then our environments tends to respond in a negative manner. And if we are in tune with our surroundings then our environment is far more positive. This makes perfect sense when we consider the polar opposites. If we are constantly impatient or aggressive towards others what tends to happen? You got it; people tend to be more aggressive towards us. During my time as a youth worker I was constantly reminded of this fact when dealing with young people with antisocial behavioural difficulties. More often than not if we go around looking for trouble we normally find it comes our way! Therefore the constant rule of the 'Universal Law' states that cause and effect are in perfect balance and that if we create negative causes we reap negative rewards just as we create positive causes we reap positive rewards, chanting enables us to do this in the everyday world.

When we chant we create all the right causes to enable the right effects. Consequently we go into the world with a greater amount of positive energy which always, without fail, attracts more positive energy which becomes a virtuous circle, the more we do, the more in tune we are with our surroundings and the more positively our surroundings respond. So as we become less stressed and our aggressive nature is no longer present then we will find that other people cannot help but respond to us in a far more positive manner. This tends to put us in an even better mood, or higher life-state that leads to greater and greater benefits. Subsequently our life becomes a mirror of our life-state. Chanting enables us to do this.

Also by utilising a Buddhist chant you are not externalising your focus in terms of praying to some deity of some kind or super God-like being. No, Buddhist philosophy is not about that at all, it's all about self-empowerment. Buddhist thought teaches that it's not about what anybody else does; it's about what you do! Your fate is not decided by some all powerful being but by your own actions. In other words it's nobody else's 'fault' for the circumstances you find yourself in but your own actions that have created the situations and environments that you find yourself in! To paraphrase Oliver Hardy *"That's another fine mess I've gotten myself into!"* It's all about the all powerful, all knowing Guru that is inside you 24/7. You don't need to search far to find Guru-U, but you may well have to listen very hard to that inner knowing voice and allow it to reshape your karma to create the circumstances where you can be fulfilled and content with your unique purpose and truly reveal your reason for being.

1.39 Tai Chi and Qi Gong

Tai literally means movement and Chi our energy, therefore Tai Chi is the practice of moving ones energies. Tai Chi originated in China over two thousand years ago and is thought to derive from ancient Martial Arts as a way of utilising your own and your opponent's energy. Once more, Tai Chi is rooted in the belief that there exists a universal energy, Chi, and that we are an integral part of that cosmic energy. Tai Chi is a way to balance our own energy to be in harmony with this universal energy.

When you first begin to learn Tai Chi you are given very simple movements and visualisations as to what type of energy is being created (flowing like water or firm like the earth or blowing like clouds in the wind). This creates Chi energy which is surprisingly easy to measure. All you need to do is stand and place your palms a couple of inches apart and feel the energy coming from your hands, it's a lot like the repulsion between two opposing magnets. Over time this energy can be felt when your hands are further apart. It feels a bit like you are holding a solid ball in your hands, ranging from cannonball size to basketball size. After a while this ball becomes larger and larger until you can feel the 'bounce' even when your arms are fully outstretched! So, imagine what you can now do with that energy? It is literally a very real physical energy.

Qi Gong (Qi is another way of saying Chi) is very similar to Tai Chi in many ways but differs as do certain different Martial Arts. It is a style for developing ones positive or healing Chi, and negating ones negative, or sickness, Chi. The main differences are in the stances and forms the exercises take but also in the subtleties of the concentration of the visualisations. Qi Gong goes into a lot more detail as to specifically what acupuncture meridians are being stimulated and the lessening of one's Chi rather than the building or increasing it. The essence of Qi Gong states that we, particularly in the West, have too much rising energy (Yang) which can result in sickness Chi where an energy blockage in the energy pathways is caused resulting in illness or disease. Qi Gong exercises help to move that energy block and create a smooth flow of Chi by getting rid of the excess sickness Chi. It's a lot like the benefits of acupuncture, but without the needles. This movement of Chi can and often does, result in actual physical twitches and jerks when performing the exercise. It is a most peculiar, but satisfying, sensation.

Both Tai Chi and Qi Gong are not something that you can merely read about to realise their benefits, they have to be performed to actualise your understanding. They are not a passive understanding, action has to come first and by taking that action in the form of exercises you reap the rewards. But again, they are a skill that you can only acquire through training with a qualified Master. Find one, and enrich your lives!

1.40 Other examples

Stress relief and the practices associated with stress reduction and preventative medicine are so vast in number that it would be impossible here to mention more than just a few. This list of ways of tackling the stress reduction equation is as endless as the ways that stress is caused. My advice is, as before, if you feel the need to find out more then do so! I find that exploring with an open mind and being open to ideas is as refreshing as actually taking part in these practices. Anyway, in no particular order, here are a few more ideas that you may well wish to consider;

Shiatsu – In simple terms Shiatsu is the combination of both acupuncture and massage. The term acupressure is used as a way of explaining how the use of gentle pressure applied to the acupuncture points can stimulate the Chi energy.

Reiki – Is used to stimulate the Chi energy without actually touching the body. The Reiki practitioner moves their hands over the patients' body and by using their own Chi they can stimulate the other persons Chi. Experienced practitioners have developed specific exercises in which to build positive Chi and disperse negative Chi (similar to Tai Chi and Qi Gong movements).

Indian Head Massage – As it sounds Indian Head Massage concerns itself primarily with intensively massaging the head and scalp. However, all parts of the head are massaged starting with the neck muscles and ending with all the face muscles. It can be, at its best, extremely relaxing and revitalising, it can however be administered quite roughly (especially in India) which can leave you feeling a little battered and bruised! A must if you haven't tried it before though.

Reflexology – This is a technique used for treating certain conditions through massaging the feet. It is believed that the feet contain all the end points of all the meridians, or the channels in which the Chi flows and by stimulating them through massage and acupressure the corresponding points in the body will be healed.

Chakras – There are believed to be seven Chakras, or energy centres, that run through the body from the top of the head right down to the tip of the spine. These energy centres can be stimulated through colour visualisation and by Reiki like movements. (They can also be stimulated by crystals – see next section.) The Chakras are connected to specific organs and functions of the body.

Crystals – It is believed that crystals contain healing earth energies and when placed in particular places on the body (particularly the Chakras) they can help to heal those areas connected. Crystals can also be used to detect auras and depletions of energy when used as a pendulum.

Faith Healing – Some people would say that all healing is a matter of faith. Faith in the doctors and their expertise as well as faith in the medicines that we take (or don't, as in the placebo effect). There are as many faith healers as there are beliefs. The important thing is to believe that you are going to be well and you stand a far better chance of becoming well than vice versa.

PART 2

EMOTIONAL

For many years having run my own training and development consultancy across a wide range of classic disciplines from improving communications within teams to creating efficiencies within manufacturing processes through 'lean' manufacturing, the main factor to initiate improvements, from 'on the line' production staff all the way up to the boardroom, is that of behavioural change.

I have found, on countless occasions, so many that I now no longer consider it as mere coincidence, that it is our attitude which reflects whether we are competent or not rather than simply if we have gained sufficient qualifications and experiences. To paraphrase Henry Ford; if a person has a 'can do' attitude, they normally can. If they believe that they can't, they normally don't.

The thing about attitude is that is directly linked to something we can change, something that we all have a degree of control over; our behaviour. But in order for us to change our behaviour we must first have an acute understanding of those behaviours that create inefficiencies and hold us back and therefore those things that we have to change. This normally involves a combination of direct feedback from others as well as a process of self-reflection.

Have you ever done a psychometric evaluation? These normally consist of a list of questions relating to your work or personality type in order to produce a report detailing your preferences i.e. whether you are an introvert or extrovert, an ideas instigator, resource investigator, or a completer finisher.

These tests then determine how best to establish a balanced team with as many differing personality types as possible as it is well known that the best teams are those that are made up of complementary skills in that there is no point in have a team of introverted ideas people without having people to implement, complete and finish. You will never see a football team with just Goal Keepers or just Strikers will you?

However, although extremely valuable, well proven and documented, most psychometrics tend to lack any perceptive detail as to *why* we are inclined to be the way that we are. They tell us *what* we are and then leave it at that, which to me has always felt unsatisfactory, for if we are going to affect any long lasting change in our behaviour surely we have to know what aspects we need to modify? This in turn leads us towards needing to know what those underlying motivators are as to why we have chosen to adopt certain behavioural mechanisms. So when requested by clients for their staff to undergo psychometric evaluations I can't but help feel that surely a better mechanism could be employed, that was when I started studying Emotional Intelligence.

You know when you study something and that every revelation that you have concurs with something that you have somehow known for ages? Where you are eager to turn every page because you have a deep connection and resonance with what you are studying? Where you have the realisation that you've learned this before? Well, that's exactly what happened to me when I first started reading about Emotional Intelligence. The more I studied and read the more I realised that something that I'd known for a long time that was supposedly 'cutting edge' and a new way of understanding. This was something that I had somehow intuitively known all along but never been able to fully articulate. After all some do say that we learn most what we need to know. Finally it had a name, and that name was the Emotional Quotient, or EQ. Some people also call it 'the common sense quotient'.

Most people are familiar with the concept of IQ, i.e. our Intelligence Quotient. This is the standard measure of our cognitive abilities which, like a psychometric evaluation also takes the form of a list of questions and exercises designed to determine how well we process information. But that is where it begins and ends; in our heads, as IQ is primarily focused towards our capacity to process information and our cognitive abilities but it has absolutely nothing to do with our relationships and how well we get on with others.

However, EQ is all about understanding ourselves as well as how we understand others, how we come across to others as well as how we relate to them. Also, another fundamental difference between IQ and EQ is that over time our IQ has the inevitable tendency to decrease which is why when you undergo an IQ test you are always required to state your age as you are then compared with the group norm for that age group. But our EQ tends to increase over time as its primarily behavioural, which is something we have the capacity to change for the better. We cannot change our cognitive function but we can change our behaviour, therefore our attitude which, as the old saying goes, determines our altitude!

As we move into this hugely significant section I will refer to the, what is known as, **realms of emotional intelligence** including the basic subcomponent parts known as the sub-scales. These realms, in bold, and subscales are:

1. The Intrapersonal Realm – how well you understand yourself.
Self Regard – the ability to respect and accept yourself as basically good.
Emotional Self-Awareness – the ability to recognise your feelings.
Assertiveness – the ability to express your feelings.
Independence – the ability to be free of emotional dependence.
Self-Actualisation – the ability to realise your potential capabilities.

2. The Interpersonal Realm – how well you understand others.
Empathy – to be aware of and appreciate the thoughts and feelings of others.
Social Responsibility – the ability to demonstrate that you are a co-operative member of a social group.
Interpersonal Relationships – the ability to establish and maintain mutually satisfying relationships.

3. The Adaptability Realm – how well you size up, respond and modify your behaviours.
Reality Testing – the ability to assess between what is subjectively experienced and what objectively exists.
Flexibility – the ability to adjust your emotions, thoughts and behaviours.
Problem Solving – the ability to identify and define problems as well as to generate and implement effective solutions.

4. The Stress Management Realm – how you cope as part of a team/partnership.
Stress Tolerance – the ability to withstand adverse events without caving in.
Impulse Control – the ability to resist or delay an impulse, drive or temptation to act.

5. The General Mood Realm – your general outlook on life
Optimism – to look on the brighter side of life and maintain a positive attitude.
Happiness – the ability to feel satisfied, to enjoy yourself and others and to have fun.

Figure 5 : Emotional Intelligence Realms

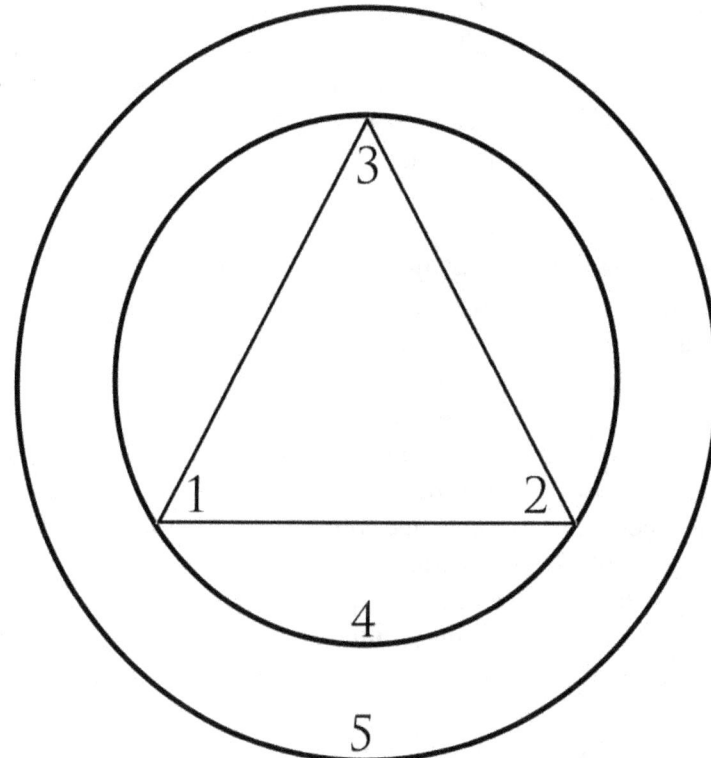

1. Intrapersonal – understanding yourself better not only leads to greater awareness and greater actualisation but also towards the notion of wanting to understand others better.
2. Interpersonal – when you want to understand others better your relationships with them improve.
3. Adaptability – when your relationships with others are improved and you have a greater understanding of what they want/need/require as well as knowing what makes you tick, you will find that you are far more flexible in your approach with regards to the relationships you have, be it at work or at home.
4. Stress management – when you have better relationships with people you reduce your stress levels considerably.
5. General Mood – when you are less stressed you are happier, more tolerant and optimistic.

What I like about this model is that it also works in reverse. If you are more hopeful, optimistic and happier you tend to better equipped to deal with stress which usually means that you have a wide repertoire of behavioural responses. Adaptability is linked to empathy and if you have an inclination towards what makes other people perform to their best then you normally have the same inclination towards understanding yourself.

Having an understanding of these components gives us a far greater understanding into, not only what makes us tick and why we have certain preferences, but also what these preferences are in others. Consequently EQ gives us a greater awareness as to how to create balance within ourselves as well as within the dynamics of our relationships with others which is a far greater indicator of how successful we will be in life rather than merely our ability to reason by collecting facts and figures and our cognitive function. Possessing intellect does not always guarantee success as it is often sadly the case that the greater the intellect the poorer the communications skills. Establishing and maintaining mutually satisfying relationships with others is normally a more reliable mechanism towards predicting success in life. Or to put it another way, we don't have to be a genius to get on in life, we can get on in life simply by getting on with others.

The science of emotional intelligence, i.e. the proven, peer corroborated, published and independently verified evidenced based conclusions, has now given us a far greater insight into how our emotions govern our behaviour. More recently, with the advent of more powerful MRI (Magnetic Resonance Imaging) machines and the cognitive research into the areas of the brain that elicit emotional responses, scientists are beginning to reach the conclusion that our emotions in fact have a far greater contribution to our decision making process than first believed.

Current understanding states that we think and rationalise before we decide to act. However recent evidence suggests that our brains work in a complete different way in that we emotionally react first (as these parts of the brain are closer together therefore it's actually quicker) and then rationalise second as these parts of the brain are more widely dispersed. People have called it gut instinct; but in reality it's actually brain instinct and it's something we've been doing this from the beginning of our evolution and for countless generations as a matter of pure survival. Far better to react first and think about it later than end up as someone's supper!

Another example of a subconscious process that we have unknowingly tapped into for generations is something known as The Human Givens. The science of Human Givens is all about assessing the needs of human beings in order to create balanced individuals (and in turn a balanced society) and stems from work in psychiatry where a list of our basic human needs are translated into a list of 'givens' i.e. it is a given that when we buy a car that it will come with four wheels, or it is a given that spring always follows winter. The Human Givens approach is that we all have a list of givens and unless they are met, in full, we are somehow depleted and unable to create balance in our lives. Psychiatry goes a step further by claiming this to be at the root of many (if not all) psychiatric conditions, ranging from mild depression right up to psychosis and paranoid schizophrenia. Think about the trail of destruction that is left in people's lives, as well as in the lives of their friends, family and colleagues, who suffer from these conditions and illnesses.

This research has spread to encompass the realms of education and personal development, in fact there is now a whole educational movement dedicated to teaching coming from the Human Givens perspective i.e. if a child is deprived any of the Human Givens their development will inevitably suffer.

So what are these Human Givens? The list is far too exhaustive to expand upon here, but I trust that those inclined to leaving no stone unturned will do their own research as there is now a whole plethora of information via the internet. But for the purposes of this book and its central theme I will include one or two examples, the first being that of **Attention** – both to give and receive. Two things here, have you ever noticed how much better you feel when someone is actually listening to you? When all of your thoughts and ideas are appreciated. And second how much worse you feel when no one is listening to you at all? When all your ideas are ridiculed. So which is better?

Here's a great example about the Human Given of Attention. During the Middle Ages the Emperor of Germany and Sicily, Frederick the second, had an idea. He wondered, would babies born in Germany naturally speak German and would babies born in Italy naturally speak Italian? So he devised a plan, and the plan entailed getting a group of both Italian and German babies (I shudder to think how he actually went about this!) and let them grow up having not been spoken to. So he gave strict instructions to their nurses only to administer to their basic needs (very much like Maslow's, food, warmth, shelter etc.) but not to communicate with them in any way.

What do you think happened? Did they grow up not communicating? Did they create a language of their own? Did chaos ensue? Neither. The experiment failed within eighteen months as all the babies died. They were literally starved of attention!

Another pertinent example of Human Givens is the need for **Purpose** – to believe that our lives have meaning. How much better do we feel when we are involved in a worthwhile task where we embrace challenges and set ourselves worthwhile tasks? Where we have a sense of absorption in that task and we achieve that state of 'Flow' where time seems to speed by? Don't we feel good? Don't we feel refreshed rather than exhausted? Don't we feel equilibrium?

Once again, there are three principles for maintaining emotional balance which are:

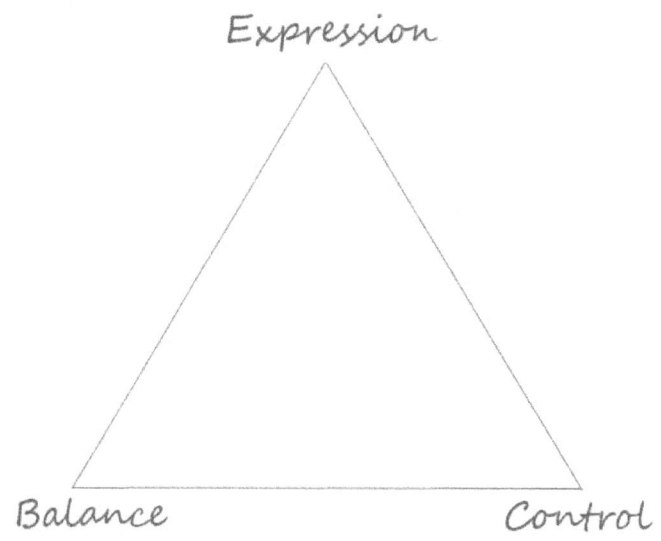

Figure 6 : Emotional Balance

The Emotional Expression section will consider such topics as how to explore and understand your emotions as well as discussing which emotions are considered as appropriate or inappropriate. Which emotions are considered positive and which are considered destructive and under what circumstances they are considered so. This section will also consider emotional expressions such as Anger/Rage the argument of Nature verse Nurture i.e. are you born with these tendencies or do you learn them? We will also cover the necessity of talking and communication and exploding the myth as to why it's considered wrong for men to cry. We will also look at the importance of good humour.

The Balance section discusses Ego, Self and Others as well as the important roles that Love, Money, Sex and Sleep play in creating balance in your life.

In the section on Control Guru-U explores 'The Illusion of Control' and how you should aim towards emotional equilibrium. This section also discusses Perseverance, Irritability/Annoyance as well as some suggested techniques for maintaining your composure during difficult challenges.

EXPRESSION

To express one's emotions in a constructive and appropriate manner is not only the mark of a balanced individual, but also the mark of a balanced society. Therefore to express one's emotions in a destructive and inappropriate manner is not only the definition of an unbalanced individual and also the description of a society in chaos. Our emotions and the expression of our emotions are the true marks of civilisation and a powerful example of the uniqueness of human expression. Therefore in order for any society to progress in a positive and constructive way we must first of all learn, as individuals, to fully understand our emotions far better in order to deal with them more positively.

The individual is society in microcosm. Society is the individual in macrocosm. Without emotional equilibrium within the individual how can we possibly have equilibrium within society? If our physical aspects are the cornerstones of us as balanced and confident individuals, our emotions are the cornerstones of creating a balanced and tolerant society, the implications are that far fetching. The case of Derek Bird comes to mind and the shootings in Cumbria in 2010. Here was a person whose emotions were so out of control and imbalanced he went on a three hour killing spree before eventually turning the gun on himself. His internal conflict turned outward – and why is it always men who commit these types of atrocities?

Without balance in the emotional aspects of our lives we are like a ship sailing without a compass where we are bound to smash into the rocks sooner or later. Therefore it is essential that we must try to understand the fundamentals of our own emotional stability. Some people say that they have got their emotions 'under control', which is not always a healthy state to be in as it usually means they are suppressing them, whilst others wear their emotions on their sleeves and tend to be desperately unhappy. So we must strike the right balance between being aware of our emotions, whilst allowing ourselves to express our emotions constructively.

But what does it mean to have equilibrium within our emotions? It would help here to have the dictionary definition of the word equilibrium: *'A state of rest produced by counteraction of forces; balance'*. Again the word balance crops up. Therefore, quite literally, it means that in order for us to balance our emotions we must first learn to recognise and to counteract the forces that impact on our emotional state. But how do we go about doing that? We can't very well take our emotions out and weigh them, can we? So we must find a way of first *quantifying* our emotions. The easiest way to quantify our emotions, apart from conducting your own EQi (Emotional Quotient Inventory), would be to categorise them as positive or negative, appropriate or inappropriate.

As an example, let's say that you are dining out and the waiter keeps bringing you the wrong order. First of all you decide whether or not to complain. Naturally you don't wish to make a fuss (especially if you are British!) but you know if you don't say anything you will only be suppressing your emotions as well as eating something that you find distasteful, so you decide to have a quiet word. Now, if the waiter is doing his job properly he will probably apologise for the error and try to rectify it to your satisfaction. However, when he returns, the order is still wrong. So do you blow up or try a different strategy? This question is based on what your Guru inside considers to be the most appropriate form of action. It's that inner guiding voice that will tell you which the right course of action to take is. Its innate wisdom will inform you as to whether your actions are appropriate or inappropriate. In this situation anger would certainly seem to be inappropriate as it would only make the situation worse. A solution would probably be to call for the manager, without offending the person who is about to serve you a meal (which is always a dangerous thing to do!)

Take another situation where the extreme emotion of anger would actually be considered as appropriate. We often consider anger to be primarily destructive but it is like any of the other arsenal of emotions that we have at our disposal and if used appropriately can indeed be a formidable weapon. For example if a friend or a loved one was wrongly accused of a crime and falsely imprisoned it would be appropriate to be completely angered by this injustice and would certainly lead us to take appropriate action on their behalf. But it certainly would not be appropriate to shout and scream at the judge for example. Once we learn to listen to Guru-U we learn to tap into our emotions and in turn develop a higher sense of what is appropriate and what is not. Once we trust our Guru inside it will give us the best advice as to when to manifest our anger and when to mask it. It's all a matter of trust. Trust in our Gurus wisdom and trust in our own actions and reactions.

Our emotions are reactions to a 'list' of deep-seated beliefs and values as to what we consider as appropriate and what we do not. From the very first moment of our waking existence we have all been conditioned as to what is acceptable and what is not. Look at any parent of a small child, especially a toddler, and listen to how many times they say 'No'. It is literally hundreds of times per day as the child explores its new and unfamiliar environment. What it can touch and what it cannot. OK, in the case of a small child this is primarily for its own safety but we will explore the nature/nurture argument in greater detail in this section as well as other factors including the physiological causes and effects that our emotions have on us. We will also look at understanding our own and other people's emotions and the nature and complexities of mood swings and other emotional disorders.

Suppression of one's emotions is one of the most insidious aspects of modern times and has undoubtedly led to countless breakdowns, both nervous and relationship, as well as the unfortunate extremes of numerous suicides and murders. The lessons learned are that suppressing one's emotions is merely a temporary solution which inevitably has drastic consequences. Our whole psyche is based on the expression of our emotions not the suppression. The relationship between our conscious mind and our subconscious mind is primordial and dates back to man's earliest development and to tamper with these fundamental aspects of our makeup is to court disaster. Modern man is a strange animal indeed. On the one hand we are reasonable and rational whilst on the other brutish and unstable where seemingly small things can spark a major incident. Anyone who has experienced major family upheavals on Christmas Day or at a wedding can testify to this point.

Therefore, in order to express your emotions constructively you must first reach a level of understanding and appreciation as to what they are, why you have them and to what good you can direct them.

2.11 Exploration

"Resolve to be thyself; and know that he, who finds himself, loses his misery." Matthew Arnold.

In order for us to fully understand our emotions we must first explore them in greater detail. However, most people, for one reason or another, consciously choose not to have to delve into these deeper aspects of their lives.

But why is that? As a behaviouralist I have found a very simple explanation, the most deep seated of them all; the fear of change and uncertainty! Our ancient primeval brain, located in the brain stem is basically a frightened animal for our most basic survival needs; fight, flight & freeze.

I recently read an explanation to an experience that we have probably all had at some point in the past, that of falling asleep (and it's usually on the bus or train, or even in a lecture, wherever there are other people to witness your humiliation) very very quickly and then all of a sudden you have that "Whoa!" moment. Your head snaps back and you're wide awake. Sometimes this happens when we are really tired and either in bed, or even your favourite chair, you seem to plunge into sleep and, Bang! You get a strange falling like feeling. Do you know what that is? It's the hypothalamus triggering the most basic of our human reactions, that of the grabbing mechanism. I love this explanation as we tend to convince ourselves that as human beings we are so advanced yet there lies in our brains a mechanism to prevent us from falling out of trees! Have you ever wondered why we use such terms as dropping off, or falling when we refer to how we go to sleep?

Therefore this essential aspect of our ancient behavioural mechanism still has a powerful influence over how we react to a given set of circumstances, another one of which is the fear of change. Our primordial mind says "Change is bad", change equals uncertainty and uncertainty illicits fear. Therefore we fear change. Consequently we choose not to delve into the uncertainty of our inner selves.

But that's pretty lame, because it's easier not to most people tend not to. The same could be said about diet and exercise which is why most people choose not to, because it's just too hard and look at the consequences of the chronic lack of exercise and poor diets are having on the health of our nations. The same is true with your emotions. Once you have got to grips with the fundamental nature of your feelings you can move forward towards a bright and prosperous future. This is, in terms of EQ the Intrapersonal Realm, the realm where you really get to know yourself for what you are, 'warts and all'.

The first step that we can take in order to improve our EQ is the Intrapersonal realm – how well we know ourselves. Over the years we have all buried deep in our subconscious minds all the unpleasant things that, not only do we not wish to discuss, we don't even want to think about. Consequently we seem to go round and round in circles constantly being reminded of those problems that we wish to forget. The reason for this is because the subconscious mind is like a small child who is always asking "Why?" And if all you ever say to that child "I don't want to talk about it." It will always wonder "Why?" And before you know it will again be asking "Why?" As in the words of Ogden Nash;

"A child need not be very clever to learn that 'later dear' means never!"

Until you break free from this vicious cycle you can never move forward. You will always keep coming around to the same old problems. Once and for all you must be able to answer the question as to why you are perpetuating these situations and circumstances and nine times out of ten it will because you have brushed certain things under the carpet that you were not ready to deal with at that time. But the more you brush things under the carpet the greater the chance that they will trip you up. And it's no good blaming anyone else when rubbing your grazed knees when it was you all along!

Now is the time for you to face up to all of your situations and circumstances and take full responsibility for both your actions and thoughts. It is the time to really get to know yourself and finally take complete responsibility for all of your emotions because once you do you need never look on your emotions as an enemy ready to strike you down in an instant, but as an ally and trusted friend who will aid you over life's obstacles one by one. Have you ever witnessed an army assault course with a team of recruits going over it? To complete it successfully they must all work together as a team as some of the obstacles are completely impossible to conquer alone. You must consider your emotions in exactly the same way. They are all members of the same team with the same objectives in mind, much like The Human Givens. They are meant to be there in order to enable you to surmount the seemingly impossible assault course of life and for you to succeed! Each emotion has its part to play and each is as important as the next for even anger, when used appropriately has its own unique function.

2.12 In touch, not out of touch

"The trick is in what one emphasises. We either make ourselves miserable, or we make ourselves happy. The amount of work is the same." Carlos Castaneda.

So, what does it mean to be 'in touch' with our emotions? It's probably easier to describe someone who is 'out of touch' with his or her emotions in order to illustrate the point more clearly. A person who is out of touch with their emotions will often feel as if their emotions are 'controlling' them which can result in them feeling a sense of anxiety and low self-worth and possibly suffering from 'panic attacks' without ever really being able to put their finger on the reasons why they are feeling that way in the first place. This often leads these people into a debilitating downward spiral of emotional confusion resulting in increased stress (poor stress management), lower self worth (lack of self actualisation), strains in their personal as well as work relationships (interpersonal relationships) and in some cases, can even result in a complete nervous breakdown and the total lack of will to carry on living at all (intrapersonal relationships, general mood, happiness and optimism) for no one who is optimistic contemplates suicide as they invariably possess hope for the future even, and often especially, during testing times.

Our emotions are like a pressure regulator where we can all 'only take so much' and then we have to 'let off steam'. For some this comes in the form of recreation (playing sport or taking a well-earned holiday). For some this increased pressure manifests itself as lack of patience, short temper and angry flare-ups. For others it can simply lead to breaking down in tears for seemingly no apparent reason (impulse control). This is because their pressure levels are so high and they have not yet found a way of reducing that pressure. More often than not people suffering from this type of stress and anxiety are not even aware that they are suffering from it at all and they go from one bout of anxiety and depression to the next without ever really knowing why or even understanding what the fundamental underlying causes are in the first place. Finally, usually after receiving advice from a friend, family member or colleague, they decide to visit their GP who, more often than not, prescribes pharmaceutical drugs such as Prozac or 'Beta Blockers'. Unfortunately, as with a lot of Western medicine therapies, this merely masks the *effects* of the problem rather than tackling the root *causes*. This is what being in touch with our emotions is all about, tackling the root causes of our stresses and anxieties rather than denying that they exist at all.

To be in touch we have to be willing and able to consider a great many factors such as our upbringing, our parental and social peer group influences, our beliefs and values as well as our expectations in order to reach any satisfactory conclusions. Primarily however, we must first do the most obvious and sometimes the most painful thing and that is to be completely honest with ourselves because, let's face it, if we can't be honest with ourselves then how can we ever truly be honest with anyone else? This is one of modern mans most pressing paradoxes. We live in a world where we are more and more dependent on our fellow man for virtually everything that we require (food, heat, transport, clothing, etc.) and yet we still cannot be completely honest with others as we are still not able to be honest with ourselves, why is that? I believe that this is a self-protection mechanism that we have learned as a coping strategy so that we don't have to expose the more unpleasant aspects of our natures such as what we have considered previously regarding fear of uncertainty. Unfortunately this is where we seem to go wrong, we pretend that these so-called 'negative emotions' play no part what so ever in our emotional make-up, wrong! The reason for the whole gamut of our emotions only becomes clear when we start to explore what they really are and what their function really is.

2.13 Negative/ Positive

"All experience is an arch to build upon." Henry Brooks Adams.

Up to now we have been looking at the negative effects when our emotions are out of balance and are unstable, fortunately, our emotions are not always negative and controlling but they can also be positive as well as inspiring! Let's face it, our emotions, and our emotional expressions are truly what make us human. They are the basis of all the greatest works of art, poetry, music and much more besides the need for mere procreation. Our emotions are what drive us towards fulfilling all of our cherished wants, needs and desires. The world would be a much colder place if we were not to express ourselves, would it not? Can you imagine a world without love and passion and tears of joy? These are the things that raise human beings above all other sentient life forms, our gift of expression. Without expression there would be no Fifth Symphony, no Stairway to Heaven, no Golden Gate Bridge, no Aston Martin DB9 and no Romeo & Juliet.

Emotions, and the expression of our emotions, are a uniquely human trait. Yes we know animals can feel pain and pleasure but they are the base emotions that we share. No, we as human beings possess a far greater spectrum of emotions as we do linguistically. We base our ability to communicate and to build as being uniquely human; I also believe that our emotion intelligence is what truly defines us as unique. What I find amazing about this concept is that we can now allow ourselves to completely open ourselves up to experience as many positive emotional experiences as we can in our oh so short life-spans and thereby enrich our own existence by doing so. Emotions are now not something to be ignored but to be embraced at every single opportunity to create an existence where everything tastes fresh and new and where everyday holds countless possibilities.

This is our purpose, our reason for being, to be human and to live a life overflowing with radiance. We are not meant to live as shallow vessels by limiting our potentials. We are each unique, beautiful creatures fulfilling our own unique purpose. To be alive and to experience all that life can throw at you, good or bad, and to know it, and accept it, for what it is. To quote Kipling *"If you can keep your head, when all about you are losing theirs..."* This is the essence of our very humanity. To live at peace with oneself and all around you. Just as the bones of the feet, in evolutionary terms, are ideally suited to running our emotional intellect is also evolving to an infinite point. There has to be a scientific and empirical reason as to why evolution has chosen to go out of its way to dedicate so much time in the development of our emotions. Let's face it; evolution happens for very specific reasons, so why bother if it wasn't going to be put to some use? Why have emotions at all? Why not be like cats or cattle? Could it be that we are meant to be more than that? And could it not also be that to fulfil our purpose as human beings that we are meant to recognise and celebrate the existence of the 'divine' gift of our emotions? I imagine our emotions to be like the individual instruments in an orchestra, and we the conductor. We can either create a cacophony or a symphony, it's all about trying.

There is a Buddhist saying that goes *"Our earthly desires are our enlightenment."* And by this it means that the very things that make us human, our emotions, and the expression and experience of our emotions is a high and lofty place. It puts us in a place above everyday existence, a place where we are in direct contact with our divinity. It is a place where our inner Guru, that all knowing being, resides. It is a vast storehouse of all we have ever done and experienced that can be tapped into at our will to make all future experiences not only extremely pleasurable at one end of the spectrum, but also to make more bearable at the other.

And then, as it often does, shit happens! Because life also has a way of doing that doesn't it? One minute it's clear sailing, and the next you're capsizing in a hurricane. So how do we deal with our emotions at that point I hear you ask?

2.14 Anger/Rage

> *"Anger has long been regarded as a basic element of affective life, a fundamental or primary human emotion. It is crucial for human survival, having important internal regulatory and social communicative functions. Physiologically, it prepares the body to initiate and sustain high levels of focused and directed activity. Psychologically, it is linked to self-protection and aggressive action tendencies. As a form of social communication, anger conveys distinct messages to others, forecasting predictable consequences, and eliciting affective and behavioural responses in others."*
> Craig Sternberg and Joseph Campos.

Let's look at one of the most extreme negative emotional expressions and then explore the issues around manifesting anger and rage as well as its causes and its effects. During my work as a youth care worker I saw, all too often, the downward (or in terms of chi, upward) spiral from anger to rage. Unfortunately for these young people it has become a mechanism designed to elicit a response, (especially in Attention Deficit Hyperactivity Disorder, ADHD) where these unfortunate young people believe that any attention, as in our basic Human Givens, is better than none at all. The root causes of this are all too often them being either ignored as a child, under-stimulated or in the worse cases ridiculed or even physically beaten. (See nature/nurture later).

In the case of these young people and with others who suffer from anger we often advise them to take some form of anger management training and explore the root causes of their angry outbursts and consider other strategies to use rather than primarily resorting to anger. The first step is always to look back at their angry episodes and discuss what took place prior to the episode in an attempt to find the triggers to their anger. Once these triggers have been identified we then prescribe various methods to enable them to deal with similar events in the future in a different and less destructive manner. The classic being the proverbial count to ten where they are asked to recognise when their 'hot button' has been pressed and to realise that their next actions are the most important, i.e. to 'blow up' or 'cool down' to 'wade in' or to walk away. I constantly use the saying "If you change your reaction to a situation then you change the outcome". Let's face it, our reactions are probably the only aspects of situations that we have any control of as we often feel that we are victims of situations and circumstances beyond our control; the train was late, the boss was angry and rude, the kids have made a mess. Although we seemingly have no control over circumstances there is only one person who has control over our reactions and that is the person we look at in the mirror, therefore the only person who can empower or disempower us, is us. And the only person who observes our behaviour and reactions is Guru-U.

Often these angry tendencies are rooted deep in our lives and take more than the simple idea of counting to ten and then reacting in a different manner. In extreme cases some people may well have been expressing anger and manifesting rage for a very long time indeed, especially with older 'patients' as they may well have been behaving this way for a great many years. In these cases we have to look back into their pasts and uncover the reasons as to why they have always chosen to act in this manner and also, most importantly, the outcomes their actions have created. This is where, almost without a single exception, we recognise that their anger has become destructive and does not serve to help them out of these situations, rather, it makes them a whole lot worse and often leads to increasing episodes of anger and rage and into a downward spiral of events. Many scientific tests have been carried out regarding this and it has been proven that the more we manifest anger the more anger and situations with the potential to trigger our anger occur in our lives. It's a lot like smiling in reverse; the more we smile at others the more others smile at us. Therefore, the more we show anger the more others will show anger towards us; you reap exactly what you sow.

Fortunately the vast majority of people who undergo some type of anger therapy find the whole process extremely beneficial and as a result enrich and transform their lives by finally taking responsibility for their own actions by regarding the actions of others as that other persons own responsibility and to look at these in a more positive light. They become like small tests that are 'sent to try us'. I use the word therapy here in a very deliberate manner as I believe that the people who suffer from angry outbursts are, in a very real sense, suffering from a debilitating condition. Much in the same way as an addict tends to live a destructive life through not being able to control their impulses the 'anger addict' similarly suffers through lack of control and the very core of controlling any addiction is to recognise that one has a problem and then to empower oneself. Once the sufferer recognises the causes of their condition and the destructive effects their actions are having (on themselves as well as others) then they truly are on 'the road to recovery'. They have finally reached a breakthrough in their treatment when they can say to themselves "No matter what happens, I, and I alone, am responsible for myself." When they realise that no one else can tell them how to act or react then the whole process of self-empowerment kicks in, which in turn can lead to a virtuous circle and the more you do, the better you become.

Also anger, from the Human Givens perspective, is a subconscious awareness (that we are probably not even consciously aware of) that 'something is missing'. Somehow we'll feel as though something is not quite right, even though we can't actually put our fingers on it. This is the subconscious tick list that is the Human Givens. It might be that we are not receiving (and giving) enough attention. We might feel a lack of connection or community. It could be that we feel as though our life has no purpose and we are not involved in anything that could be considered as worthwhile. All of these things are like a toxic brew, they bubble and fester over the years, often without us even being aware of what is missing in the first place other than that gnawing feeling that surely there's more to life? Where the result is, lack of fulfilment, frustration, increasingly stressful situations and ultimately angry outbursts. As any doctor will tell you, in order to find the cure we must first understand the nature of the condition.

2.15 Nature/Nurture

So, it's time to look at the reasons why we all display our emotions in any particular way given a particular set of circumstances and to explore why it is that some people, given exactly the same set of circumstances, will react one way when others will react completely differently. This is primarily down to values and belief systems that we have 'inherited' from our families, as well as the effects from our respective societies, ethnic groups and gender (which we shall explore in greater detail – see 'Men shouldn't cry'). The age-old argument of Nature against Nurture goes something like this. The Nature argument says that we are all merely products of our genes and that our behavioural response is somehow hard wired into our programming. The Nurture argument states that we are all products of our environments and parental and social upbringing and whatever our actions and reactions may be they have been programmed into us by these influences. So, what of the genius in a family of illiterates? And what of the tear-away from the well adjusted family? I firmly believe that we are neither governed by our genes nor controlled by our influences but are products of each. We are all born to a given set of parents at a precise time and place and that all of these will have an influence on our potentialities and who we are and what we are likely to become. It is difficult to comprehend that the son of racists will have much racial tolerance, but not impossible, as this depends on other influences later on in life. Also, because we may be born into poverty it does not always follow that we must endure poverty for the rest of our lives.

Let us go back to the example of when we are first born. We all carry with us certain natural responses that dictate our behaviour. We cry when we need food or our nappies need changing or if we are left alone. We then, throughout the rest of our lives, modify this behaviour depending on the results we obtain. So, if the desired outcome is to receive attention and that by shouting and screaming we receive attention, and then we will inevitably tend to use that strategy when we desire attention. (It's not just young children here that I'm talking about as many 'adults' still use this type of behaviour to receive attention). Conversely, if we are shown, or taught, that different responses can lead to similar outcomes then we have at our disposal a more complete array of different tactics to employ to derive a similar outcome.

Let us look at the desire to have a loving partner in one's life. As we all know, to invite love into one's life is the one ephemeral sensation that we can neither dictate nor conjure up like magic. We cannot go out into the world and demand a partner, nor can we plead for someone to love us. It is, like with so many things in life, as in the old adage, "If it is worth anything at all, it is worth working at", we must, through hard work (and trial and error) earn the right to be loved. We have to learn about rejection before we can learn what it means to succeed and not to be put off by this fact.

> *"If you can meet with triumph and disaster and treat those two impostors just the same..."* Kipling.

So, why do some people react one way to a given situation and others react to the same situation in a completely different way? This is because they have learned to respond in a particular way given their previous experiences and outcomes based on the range of strategies that they have been exposed to. So, if a young person has only ever seen anger and upheaval in their lives they are far more likely to employ these tactics than someone who has only ever known tolerance and patience. If anything, this is where the nurture argument holds its own; however, this is not always the case as there are obvious exceptions. For instance, why is it that child prodigies, such as musical or mathematical geniuses, tend to come from families who are adept musicians or mathematicians? My partner recently informed me of another exception regarding a young child that a friend of hers had adopted. The adopted parents had obviously been vetted for suitability so that they could provide a secure and caring environment to bring up the child. However, in later years the child turned uncontrollable, reverting to its genetic behavioural characteristics. Recently geneticists have identified the gene that probably dictates a person's emotional and behavioural characteristic. Tests with twins have also shown similar results; a well adjusted child will remain well adjusted no matter what their environmental influences and a troubled child will tend to remain that way even in a relatively stable environment.

This tends to suggest that it is all a matter of nature and the genes we are born with get to dictate our emotional state throughout life. I, however, believe that this is only the case in certain circumstances and certainly not a hard and fast rule as there are far too many exceptions to this rule for it to be completely true. I believe that neither factor has dominance over the other and that each of the factors has as much influence as the other. We are neither products of our nature nor our nurture but products of both. We are products of our behavioural attitude that is imprinted in us by many means both internal and external, and as we have discussed, our behaviour is something that we have more control over than we give ourselves credit for. Invariably, this is because we rarely give credit to our Guru!

2.16 Appropriate/Inappropriate

In this section we will try to understand a little more about what are considered as appropriate emotional behaviours and what are considered inappropriate and who gets to decide what is appropriate and what is not. Are we given some kind of list or commandments that we constantly refer to? And if this appropriateness is completely dictated to us by our families, friends and other social influences alone then where did these people derive their lists from?

I believe that we are programmed from a very early age, based on a set of assumptions that we should behave in a certain way given a particular set of circumstances reflected by what we experience around us. So, for instance, if we witness flashes of anger from our parents when they are driving along the road and a car cuts them up, we will therefore believe that it is okay to react this way given a similar set of circumstances and therefore consider this as an appropriate response. Conversely if we witness care and compassion to those less fortunate then we subsequently learn to become a more caring and compassionate person. Also, if we are told that it is wrong to express oneself, either emotionally or critically, then we will tend to bottle up or suppress our feelings and opinions (see Men shouldn't cry).

These assumptions, however, could well be wrong in themselves and referring back to the word **assume**; it tends to make an **ass** out of **u** and **me**. We are setting ourselves up for a fall if we consider the assumptions and opinions of others as being one hundred percent right, one hundred percent of the time. There comes a time in our lives, usually in adolescence, that we begin to question these assumptions and feel the need to redefine the opinions of others to create our own list as to what is right or wrong, appropriate or otherwise. This is a time when the confines of nurture change, where we are no longer just influenced by our family and are replaced by our natural responses. This can also happen at other important milestones in our lives. For example, let's take someone who has lived in the shadow of an overbearing partner and has always gone with the flow as to his or her partner's assumptions, opinions and actions. They may reach a point in their relationship where they begin to think, "Hang on a minute. Maybe this person, who I have always considered to be right, is not right all of the time". For when we begin to question we start the process of needing answers and by doing so we seek out the truth. This is the process of the emergence of our Guru knowledge, when we replace someone else's 'higher' wisdom with our own.

It is usually the case that during periods of heightened emotion we become sufficiently motivated to want to change things and look at life in a completely different way. For instance the breakdown of a relationship or the death of a close friend or relative, the diagnosis of a life-threatening illness or moving house to a distant and unfamiliar place where the map that we have previously used no longer applies. We now have to explore new territories and new ideas and although in a state of seeming crisis we can use this as a great opportunity to progress and move forward. As Richard Bach so eloquently puts in his masterpiece Illusions;

"Don't be dismayed at good-byes...What the caterpillar calls the end of the world, the master calls a butterfly."

2.17 Time to Talk

"Communication is a skill that you can learn. It's like riding a bicycle or typing. If you're willing to work at it, you can rapidly improve the quality of every part of your life." Brian Tracy.

We have briefly looked at the effects of the suppression of one's emotions, let us now consider in greater detail what this actually means and the effects that this can have on both the individual and everyone else within their circle of influence as there is a lot of wisdom in the old saying "A problem shared is a problem halved". It has been shown time and time again that women are far better at talking about their emotions than men are. It wouldn't seem appropriate for a man to go out for a beer with his mates and talk about problems in their relationships or lack of fulfilment in his life. It is far more acceptable to talk about safer issues such as their jobs or sport whereas women can talk about their emotions and feelings for hours on end! This is partially due to our ancient heritage passed down from our Hunter/Gatherer existence where men were primarily involved in hunting and that not saying anything at all and staying completely quiet was absolutely necessary in order not to be heard by their prey in order for the hunt to be successful. Women, on the other hand whilst gathering were free to talk to their hearts content (including the essential ability to convey to other members of their social group the whereabouts of edible plants) and still maintain this ability to the current day. However this is not a hard and fast rule as many women also experience the inability to communicate, the rapid rise in women suffering from feelings of alienation and lowered self-esteem testifies to this point.

As we have previously discovered emotions, and especially the expression of our emotions, are ways of blowing off steam and reducing life's pressures and to not reduce these pressures is a recipe for disaster. Why is it, more often than not, that the perpetrators of hideous atrocities such as Dunblane, Hungerford, the Cumbria shootings and the Columbine High School massacres always seem to be loner types who 'always kept themselves to themselves'? Could it be that had they the opportunity to talk to someone else about their emotional challenges and problems, then they may have been better equipped to deal with these challenges in a more positive manner rather than resorting to extreme violence in order to be heard? And why is it, as mentioned earlier, that the perpetrators of these crimes against humanity or invariably men? Is there a link? I think so.

Human beings are naturally social and gregarious creatures and if this primal desire is removed then we tend to react against this in varying degrees. Some will shut themselves away from the influences of others tending to lead shallower and lonelier lives. Whereas others can overcompensate by being either too loud or brash, or in extreme cases, murderously angry and bitter. We all need the opportunity to express our feelings and emotions in order to make complete sense of them.

"No man (or woman) is an island, entire of itself; every man is a piece of the Continent, a part of the main." Donne.

Without expression all that remains is suppression and lack of fulfilment and without someone to share with all that remains is the propensity towards loneliness and bitterness and when we feel we no longer have a connection to our community (another one of the essential Human Givens) we have the perfect recipe for disaster.

I have always liked the definition of loneliness as "not being the lack of company, but the lack of intimacy" (yet another Human Given) and how much more intimate is it than to talk to another person about ones wants, needs, desires, disappointments and fulfilments? This is just about as up close and personal as it gets. This is probably one of the main reasons why men tend to keep things to themselves preferring to remain aloof as a misguided form of a show of strength whereas opening up is wrongly considered as sign of weakness. Unfortunately this has been one of the undeniable reasons which has led to one of the highest rates of suicides amongst young men. In fact next to fatalities in road accidents, suicide is the next highest killer of our young men. Why is this? Is it because that as men we find it so difficult to talk to others about our problems that we bottle it all up? Then, due to the high expectations placed on men to go out and earn a good living and to create a happy and secure house and home and by not living up to these (often impinged on us through the media) expectations, we are somehow letting everybody down? And because we cannot live with the shame we are taking our own lives in record numbers? I think so. Emotions, feelings, wants, needs and desires are meant to be expressed. Why would we have them at our disposal if they were of no use? And by not being able to explain and dissect them by talking to another we are setting ourselves, and communities, up for a costly fall. So, what are the solutions? What can we do?

2.18 Men shouldn't cry?

So, here's the argument, women are considered 'more emotional' than men and anger is seen as primarily a male characteristic. Why is this? By describing women as being more emotional what we are saying is that women display their emotions more vividly and more often than men do and that because men are less able to express their emotions they resort to manifesting anger. Unfortunately there is a lot of indisputable evidence to back this up. A whole host of studies have been carried out to validate this claim and have concluded that gender roles and what is expected of them play a significant part in determining our abilities of emotional expression. A recent report from the US states that women tend to be more expressive than men in three distinct ways:

1) modulating and the changing of facial expression,
2) gesturing,
3) rate and inflection of speech.

As we looked at in the previous section men's seeming inability to express their emotions is leading to a record number of suicides (as well as mass murders) and what men have to learn to do is to be more expressive and in touch with their feelings and emotions. Also for those of us who are parents we must learn to teach our children the importance of emotional expression and for it not to be something that we play down or even ridicule. I'm sure we have all heard the irate parent of the boy who is crying to 'stop being a big girl?' To illustrate this point I am reminded of the death of the Greek philosopher Socrates who, on his death-bed when his (male) followers began to cry at his parting stated;

"Really, my friends, what a way to behave! Why, that was my main reason for sending away the women, to prevent this sort of disturbance."

The question Stephanie A. Shields raises in her study "Speaking from the Heart" 'did Socrates admonish his companions because his companions were behaving *emotionally*, because they were behaving *like women*, or because they were behaving *emotionally like women*?

However, more recently, this aspect of our emotional expression, i.e. crying, seems to have been somewhat turned on its head. Previously, certainly during the majority of the twentieth century, it was considered as inappropriate for men to vividly express themselves and that crying, particularly in public, was considered a big no-no. On the other hand, women have been 'allowed' to cry as this is considered as being part and parcel of being a woman. But in this post September 11th era things are seemingly very different. None of us will ever forget the events of that tragic day and the aftermath in the following few days when politicians and public figures, specifically New York mayor Rudolph Giuliani and President George W Bush, were 'allowed' to reveal their tears. When they were speaking from the heart and revealing their depths of feeling they revealed their emotional authenticity and their open display of raw emotions were approved of as displaying genuineness. In fact those that were not as able to show their emotions as readily were criticised for seeming emotionally detached.

The paradox now becomes evident through the results of a recent survey that stated that in the workplace the primary reason that women are judged to have 'emotional instability' is if they cry! This is now held up as a reasonable excuse for lack of promotion or even dismissal as it summarises that if a woman were unstable she would not be professionally suitable to the added stresses and strains of executive life! So now there seems to exist a complete juxtaposition where women can no longer display their tears in public as it denotes weakness but if powerful public figures and politicians display their emotions it is considered as strength of character!

This still does not quite answer the question as whether or not men are allowed to cry or not. We have seen that it is now acceptable for public figures to cry in public, but what about your normal everyday guy? Fortunately the taboo of men not being able to cry at all, even in private, is finally being resigned to the pages of history as it seems as though 'modern-man' is allowed to express himself more freely and for the better. The 'baby-boomer' generation (born between 1945 – 1964), which has grown up in the latter half of the twentieth century have witnessed, and been part of, a dramatic shift in what has been previously considered inappropriate and what is not. This in turn has lead to a re-categorisation, known as Generation X and Generation Y.

Generation X is considered as people born just after the baby-boomer generation (circa 1965 – the early '80's) and Generation Y, those born after the 1980's who are redefining cultural and gender stereotypes. For example the new father figure is now far more involved with the hands-on upbringing of their children than they ever have been. Previously this was always considered to be the 'woman's job' and the 'man's job' was to provide the proverbial roof over the head and food on the table (hunter/gatherer). Consequently our gender stereotypes are slowly being dissolved and dismantling the purely matriarchal? Correct word? society. More and more women are a taking on professions and more and more men are assuming the role of full-time house husband and as a result becoming more and more emotionally engaged by redefining their roles. Fifty years ago, for the baby-boomer generation, this would have been considered as completely unacceptable whereas today this is considered as quite normal, so, we are progressing after all. We must, however, not allow ourselves to become complacent whist there still exists any cultural stigma placed on men's and women's emotional expressiveness.

2.19 The importance of good humour

"Good humour is a tonic for mind and body. It is the best antidote for anxiety and depression. It is a business asset. It attracts and keeps friends. It lightens human burdens. It is the direct route to serenity and contentment." Greenville Kleisser.

Going back to Sternberg and Campos's observation (2.14 – Anger/Rage) that strong emotion correlates to two distinct functions, Physiological and Psychological. I would now like to explore the physiological effect that our emotions have upon our bodies. Some would say that all we are, as human beings, is somehow a great big bag of atoms and molecules arranged in a particular pattern and that our emotions are merely 'chemical triggers' resulting in a specific response. So, when we feel good, we have chemicals such as endorphins, a natural morphine-like substance, and serotonin (which is reproduced in synthetic form as the basis for most mood enhancing medications for people suffering from conditions such as manic depression) flowing around our bloodstreams and through our brains where the receptors then pick them up and therefore influence our frame of mind. Conversely the lack of other chemicals, in this case serotonin, can adversely effect our moods creating melancholy, depression and has been found to be one of the root causes of Seasonally Affected Disorder (SAD). The other factor being the lack of sunlight during winter where light has been shown to stimulate the brain into secreting serotonin.

Clinically these observations seem correct when you consider the vast range of mood-altering prescription drugs that are now available. People suffering from psychosis must continually take their medication in order to maintain their chemical equilibrium. Children with behavioural difficulties are taking the drug Ritalin in record numbers to combat this so-called 'menace to society' to regulate their mood-swings and aggressive tendencies. I think, however, that we are missing the point and by treating these conditions from a typically western-medicine framework we are primarily treating the effects of these conditions rather than looking at the root causes.

I believe that we should accept the fact that our bodies are indeed vast medicine cabinets and that our incredibly sophisticated immune systems have the ability to heal ourselves through the appropriate use of these self regulating chemicals. In fact, consciously, we can go a step further by deliberately inducing the feel-good chemicals thereby regulating our chemical imbalances. I recently saw a TV programme that beautifully illustrates this point. It was a programme about an obscure Indian Yogic 'laughing cult' where the vast part of their exercises consisted merely of laughing! Their basis for doing this seemingly strange, yet wonderful act is that when you laugh the body secretes feel-good chemicals and the better you feel. Further western-medicine research has borne this out by proving that the more a person laughs the less likely they are to suffer for example from heart disease. Even by watching the programme I felt uplifted, in fact I ended up laughing myself. What is it about laughter that is so contagious? I suppose it's a bit like yawning in reverse. I'm sure we have all had the experience of when someone else starts to yawn it's not too long before we start yawning ourselves. The same is true with laughter, or should I say appropriate laughter as, say laughing at a funeral, is not considered as the right thing to do. But when the social construct is diminished and someone else begins to laugh, we tend to laugh with them.

Laughter is the universal tonic as it transcends all borders and ethnicities. It is a common language that we all share and a gift that we can all cherish. Not only does it have a direct impact on us socially but a positive healing effect on us physically. The more we laugh, the better we feel, and the better we feel, the more we tend to have the propensity for laughter, it is another virtuous circle. So, in order for us to regulate our negative mood swings we must take positive action and direct our focus towards feeling good and feeling good about ourselves and our very existence. It is as simple as that!

BALANCE

Although expressing our emotions is an excellent way of creating balance it is not the only aspect that we must consider when attempting to create emotional equilibrium. We must also learn that, during certain given situations, it is in fact better not to express ones emotions at all. This may seem contradictory to what we have discovered about emotional suppression but this highlights the complexities of human emotions and emotional expression. An example comes to mind where, during the course of my work as a youth care worker myself and a colleague took a young woman who had started to 'dabble' in prostitution to an outreach centre in order for her to talk to some women who had been involved in the sex industry for a number of years. We asked the young woman if she preferred for us to leave the room whilst these discussions were taking place but she said that she would actually like us to stay in the room so that we could hear what was being said in order for us all to be able to talk about it later.

So my colleague and I stayed in the room and listened to one harrowing tale after the next about 'life on the streets', drug abuse (incidentally up to 95% of sex workers take heroin, and more recently crack-cocaine, on a regular basis), violence from clients and pimps and issues around self-protection in terms of the devastating effects of HIV and AIDS (one women stated that she had lost over 25 of her close friends to AIDS). Anyway, it goes without saying that any caring human being would have found these stories disturbing, to say the least, and I am no exception. However, it certainly would have been considered inappropriate for me to fully express my emotions, other than superficially, as the whole experience was more than a little moving. Far better was for me to maintain my professionalism and remain calm and seemingly in control and then later to be able to talk about what took place without becoming 'too emotional'.

Emotional balance is not a destination to be reached but a journey to be travelled. It is an ideal state that we only arrive at for fleeting moments as even the most seemingly enlightened person is 'only human after all' and will have their good days as well as bad. I believe that what we should try to aspire to, however, is to maintain equilibrium more often than not. No one is perfect 100% of the time but, to paraphrase a Zen Buddhist saying, the pursuit of perfection is where it is at!

So, how is it that some people seem to be more balanced than others and more importantly, how do they go about creating and maintaining this balance? This next section aims to go some way towards answering these questions and more.

2.21 Ego

"The deepest craving of human nature is the need to be appreciated."
William James.

At the very centre of our emotional balance is how we view ourselves in terms of our relationships and interactions with others. Much has been written on the essence of the ego and I will not attempt here to redefine what the ego is or is not other than using the simplistic definition of our own sense of 'importantness'. We develop a sense of ourselves and how others respond to our needs very early in childhood. We initially believe that we are indeed the centres of the universe and that all things revolve around our needs, when we cry as a baby somebody usually responds. When we grow into infanthood we carry this behaviour forward and begin to 'manipulate' those around us, parents and siblings, into responding to our needs and the degree to which they respond dictates the essence and ultimately the size of our egos in later life. Unfortunately some people can carry an over-exaggerated sense of self-importance throughout the rest of their lives and are considered egotistic or possessing an over-inflated ego. Conversely, those with low self-esteem can carry a sense of self-conceit where they consider themselves and their opinions as unworthy and unimportant.

The phrase ego was first coined by the eminent psychologist Sigmund Freud who first described the ego as to mean a sense of self, but later revised it to mean a set of functions such as judgment, tolerance, reality-testing, control, planning, defence, synthesis of information, intellectual functioning, and memory, all of which go a long way towards creating a truer definition of what we would call ourselves. These are our preferred personality profiles, the way we process information, the way we act, react and justify and value our behaviours.

Obviously, in order to lead a balanced existence we all need to find our own ways to counteract these 'positive' and 'negative' forces and to accomplish the middle ground between these polar extremes. In order for us to do this we must, through the process of introspection (and in extreme cases, therapy) to analyse the causes and episodes in our lives that have created our unique individual selves. Were we nurtured as a child or ridiculed? Were our opinions listened to or ignored? Were we shown the right amount of attention in that we were listened to and our ideas and opinions were validated? Then once we have got to the root causes of the construction of our egos we can then allow our Guru to become the architect of our futures.

If we agree that we are indeed the constructs of a combination of our nature as well as our nurture we can then realise that our future ego construction is based on the causes that we make here and now in the present. If we value ourselves it is more likely that others will value us (to a point). If we value our own opinions then it is also likely that others will also value them, or at least give them due consideration rather than simple dismissing them out of hand. And if we hold on to the fact that we, and our opinions and thoughts and feelings matter, then it is merely a matter of cause and effect that others will concur.

2.22 Self

> *"Without self knowledge, without understanding the working and functions of his machine, man cannot be free, he cannot govern himself and he will always remain a slave."* G. I. Gurdjieff.

So, how do you value yourself? Do you believe that your thoughts, feelings and opinions matter? And if so, to what extent? (Intrapersonal realm of EQ) Also how much room do you leave for the thoughts, feelings and opinions of others? (Interpersonal realm of EQ) As I stated at the beginning of this section, a balanced society can only be created through the collective efforts of balanced individuals within society and not separate from it, e.g. hermits and recluses. Therefore it becomes your obligation to balance yourself first and foremost in order to live in 'the real world' to create harmony within your respective families, communities, societies and countries at large. They are like ripples in a pond that start with the splash of your own individual actions and the greater the weight of your convictions, the greater the splash and the greater the ripples. In Buddhist terminology, the greater the causes the greater the effects. Or, in more simplistic terms, if you go around creating a lot of trouble, then trouble will always result from those actions and in stark contrast, if you take your balanced self out into the world and create value from your actions then your life, and the lives of those around us, will become more enriched.

The conclusion lies in the answer to the question as to how much we value ourselves and to what extent. If, for instance we already possess a strong sense of self we must ask ourselves to what extent? Do we, for instance believe that all of our thoughts, feelings and opinions are so valuable that other peoples' are of less import? And, if so, beware, as a matter of opinion is by dictionary definition just that; *something which is open to debate!* Surely it is better to hold the views of others in equal proportion to one's own? For, does it not also follow that when we take an interest in someone else's point of view they tend to take more of an interest in ours? (To both give and receive Attention)

Why should it be that your opinion is of greater import than others are? Usually this is a matter of the belief and depth of one's own convictions and experiences. So, if we say to a child don't touch this hot piece of metal because it will burn, we know from experience that this is indisputable the case, but they however, do not and must learn this important lesson for themselves. In fact neuro scientists have now shown a direct link between our actual brain formation and painful experiences i.e. we learn as we fall and we grow as we experience pain.

In cases like these I like to use a martial arts analogy in that we are all white-belts in some things and black-belts in others. Also, if we engage in the 'fight' of life we will inevitably take some knocks and it is those very knocks that teach us what we most need to learn. When we can grade our own life experiences we can then enable ourselves to carry the weight of authority, because, let's face it, the one thing that we are all a black-belt in is in our own lives. Nobody else knows more than we do about ourselves as no one else has spent as much time with us as we have!

You are your own Guru and this knowledge and approval need not come from another source. For when you get to know yourself, and your Guru, well enough you will then begin to accept that there is still much to learn from others and you then begin the process of balancing your thoughts, feelings and opinions with the thoughts, feelings and opinions of others.

2.23 Others

"How far you go in life depends on your being tender with the young, compassionate with the aged, sympathetic with the striving, and tolerant of the weak and strong. Because some day in life you will have been all of these." George Washington Carver.

Balancing our own emotions is one thing but making sure that our emotions and feelings are in harmony with other people's moods, feelings and emotions is something else entirely. Can you imagine a world where we completely ignored the feelings of others? Picture the havoc that would be created if we sailed through the world without a single thought for anyone else. It has been said that this is one of the defining features of our humanity is our consideration and compassion for those around us. (EQ, Empathy) Anthropologists have taught us that the most successful tribes were those that could read each others moods correctly and by doing so succeeded, i.e. when to hunt together and when not to, when to display assertiveness as well as when to back down, when to fight and when to run away. On the contrary those tribes that did not possess this ability simply died out. So it's not just a simple matter of creating harmony, it is literally a matter of life and death!

Being able to read someone else's emotions is essential. Imagine for a moment what your relationship would be like if you ignored your partner's moods, feelings and emotions completely. It doesn't take long to realise that your relationship would be dead before very long does it? Imagine coming home from work in a good mood and finding your partner weeping on the phone and when they had finished their call not asking them what was wrong in case it spoiled your mood. Also imagine waking up and for no particular reason feeling very down, the proverbial 'getting up on the wrong side of the bed' and your partner not asking what was wrong, how would you feel?

The subconscious skill that we have developed in order to read other peoples emotions is as complex and myriad as our own immune systems. It is a process that has taken tens of thousands of years to reach its current point and as with all things in the process of evolution, is still progressing to a point of far greater complexity than it currently is. It is a skill that we all possess, however, as with every other skill, some possess it to a greater or lesser extent than others. Not wanting to generalise too much but women, for instance, seem to be better able to read the emotions of others than men are. As previously discussed many tests have proven that women are far more perceptive than men are when it comes to receiving the emotional signals that others transmit and, more importantly, correctly deciphering them. For example most women can read a 'false smile' or 'crocodile tears' far better than most men can.

We are all transmitters and receivers of emotions. When we transmit our emotions we encode, when we receive we decode. Whereas most men are mere beginners in the art of deciphering, most women are black belts! Even though I like to consider myself as an open-minded, observant and intuitive person I am no longer surprised that when returning home from say an evening out with my partner who is far more adept than I at reading certain aspects of the evening's proceedings and in far greater depth that I have completely missed some crucial moment. 'Did you see the look she gave him?' Again I believe that this phenomenon is rooted in our hunter/gatherer pasts where women have become more adept emotional communicators. As we have seen communication is not just a matter of words as the vast majority of our communication is non-verbal. (How we look accounts for around a staggering 55%, how we say something accounts for 38% and what we actually say only actually accounts for just 7%!) Our body language, including what we wear, facial expressions and tone of voice, including our accents, are far more precise indicators of what is being said rather than what we actually say. I think that it's obvious to us all when someone is genuine in what they say, but while con-men and manipulators still thrive, we must all accept the fact that we still have much to learn as deception is not always easily apparent.

2.24 Love

"To love a thing means wanting it to live." Confucius.

In the words of the great Tina Turner song *"What's love got to do with it?"* And why is love so important in creating balance? Because, in the words of the great Marvin Gaye, *"Only love can conquer hate."* Love is such a powerful force that it exerts its influence in virtually every aspect of our emotional make-up and therefore in its balance. For generations poets, philosophers and artists have pondered and celebrated this thing we call love, this most precious, fragile, yet enduring emotion. Imagine for a moment a life without love. Imagine the emptiness of a world without love, and when we replace it with love we can feel the richness of our existence.

Love, the feeling of being loved and the emptiness of losing love defines us as humans and unites every race, creed and colour. It knows no borders or boundaries and has been at the root of our greatest accomplishments and follies. Love exerts a powerful influence and like with any other powerful emotion if it goes unchecked it has equal power to destroy, as in the case of love turned to possessive love and jealousy, as it does to create.

Love, as a balancing force in our lives cannot be overlooked. We know that if we have love in our lives we somehow feel better than if we do not. We know that love drives us and is as much the reason as the reward for our actions. But how are we to define what love is? Is it merely the love of a partner, parent, sibling, child or friend? Or is it more than that? What about our love of natural beauty, of animals and plants? What of our love for music and objects and our love for our countries, our world and our fellow human beings? These are all the things that love is and much much more. We don't have to have a partner in our lives just to feel love or to be loved but why is it so important if we do or do not?

Love, to me, is the ultimate expression of one's desire to live. When we love someone and they love us right back our whole life seems to be somehow more enriched and we are able to face the world with greater hope and optimism where anything and everything seem possible and use that driving force to propel our lives forward with more meaning. But this is also true with the love of a cause. Those who have loved endangered species and rainforests have been driven by these causes with as much passion as lovers and have left a legacy of the creation of value and an appreciation of diversity.

Love and the expression of love is arguably a unique human trait (admittedly this also includes other mammalian species to some degree). It is a characteristic and an ideal at the same time. It is certainly a defining feature of our humanity and without a doubt a force for good in the universe. Buddhist thought states that within the universe there exists forces of good and forces of bad that are in a state of perpetual flux or 'struggle', and if left unchecked, the forces of bad (ignorance, greed, anger and stupidity) will prevail. As love is a force of good we must all learn to nurture the love we have in our lives and consciously and deliberately expand it in order to overcome negativity in the world and as 'only love can conquer hate', while hate exists we must all develop and expand our capacities to love to overcome and eradicate hate.

Once more, the case of Derek Bird comes to mind. It turns out that there was a dispute with his twin brother (his first victim) relating to a will (greed), this spilled over into the extreme of anger, rage and led to the ultimate expression of ignorance, the killing of other human beings. The ignorance that I refer to is the ignorance of our interconnectedness. As Richard Bach so eloquently puts it:

"Rarely are members of the same family born under the same roof."

2.25 Money

"Money is better than poverty, if only for financial reasons."
Woody Allen.

So, what's money got to do with creating emotional balance I hear you ask? (See above as to what disputes over money can create). For those of you who may have been fortunate enough to never have experienced financial difficulties then this may seem like a strange concept. But for probably the majority of people in the world, financial insecurity can certainly lead to a lot of worry, sleepless nights and imbalance. How many family arguments and upheavals have been caused by the lack of money? Think of the countless numbers of suicides from those that have 'lost everything' and taken the ten-storey nose-dive to the pavement as testament to this point.

A friend of mine once remarked at my resilience when I had to deal with the effects of a failed business venture. Although I was indeed deflated at losing the business I kept my head held high and dealt with the aftermath as best I could. Although I had lost many things, the relationship, the car, the house, I picked myself up, brushed myself down and 'got back on the bike' as I realised that, not only did I still possess the knowledge to create wealth and how to go about doing it, but I also now had the experience of what not to do as well as what to do (including my choice of future business partners!) "Most people would have gone to the wall by now," he said. I replied that most would have gone to the pavement, and that was not a choice I was about to make.

I recently read an excellent piece of guidance that perfectly illustrates this point. It said:

"What will the future be like? No one knows the answer to that question. All we know is that the effects that will appear in the future are all contained in the causes that are made in the present. The

important thing, therefore, is that we stand up and take action to achieve great objectives without allowing ourselves to be distracted or discouraged by immediate difficulties." Daisaku Ikeda.

In other words no matter what happens it is up to us and us alone if we allow ourselves to become discouraged or not. If we allow ourselves to be defeated, we will be, but if we choose not to, then we never will, regardless of the outcomes. In fact it is our very attitude to winning and losing that defines our successes and failures. To put it another way, if we never tried and therefore never took the risk of defeat, then we would surely fail anyway. But during testing times we also have the unique opportunity to 'turn poison into medicine' and snatch victory from the jaws of defeat! I have always loved the song from the film 'Chitty-chitty Bang-bang' that goes *"From the ashes of disaster grow the roses of success"* and I have once more created successes in my life beyond what I had previously imagined.

My friend also wisely commented that these are the very things that mark us as survivors or quitters. Not everybody possesses the fortitude to survive during a drought. Some think that it would be easier to quit life altogether rather than face an uncertain future than to be able to survive on less than a tenth of one's previous income, how lame. Others see it as simply another challenge to overcome and to get on with it without complaint, to seek new horizons and to profit from every experience.

Although the words of another song *"Money can't buy you love"* may be true it is also undeniably true that money can buy you the experiences that you love. For instance, if you love to travel (in any decent level of comfort at least) then this dream has its price tag. I know the saying that it costs nothing to walk but boots cost and if you want to walk where I live, in The Lake District, then you better have some decent waterproofs, and boy do they cost! If you have a family in pushchairs or wheelchairs and you want a holiday then you certainly can't sleep in a bus shelter. No matter what your dream, invariably it will have a price tag attached. If you love to race motorbikes or racing cars then it doesn't take a genius to work out that this doesn't come free and if you love the thrill of free falling then you had better have bought a parachute beforehand! Money, as it is often incorrectly remarked, is not the root of all evil, it's what you do with it that counts. It is only evil if you decide to buy a gun and bullets and wreak havoc! Money has no conscious volition of its own; it only becomes misdirected by those who possess it. The reverse is also true in that if you earn enough money to be able to support a worthy charitable cause where others can benefit from your fortune is this not the essence of good? Take the Bill and Melinda Gates Foundation who are aiming to eradicate diseases such as Polio and help struggling farmers succeed – how noble.

Money, and the earning of money, are outward manifestations of our motivations and actions. We learn, we apply and we are rewarded for the time taken to do so. So if we decide not to learn and not to apply then we can't complain about ending up in a dead-end job and never seeming to earn enough money just to get by. Unfortunately this is the common life experience for the vast majority. So what does it take to balance oneself in terms of money? There's not much point in reiterating that we should not live beyond our means and that we should only buy what we can afford, (one of the prime factors for the recent credit crunch) but what of dreams and ambitions? These are the things that drive us to excel and are powerful forces that need to be balanced.

I recently came across an article on the internet relating to revenue generating activities in that we all fall into either one of two categories; we either earn it or we mooch, and that these categories also split into two each; by earning it we either sell our time to someone else i.e. we have a job where someone effectively owns our time, or we run our own businesses and create value in a different way. Also with moochers we either let other people support us i.e. they have earned the money and we spend it, which is not detrimental to the other person, or we steal it, which is.

Also, there is a world of difference between what is known as speculative and consumer debt. I think the latter is obvious, the more we spend on clothes, holidays, flat screen TV's and other items that we can't necessarily afford i.e. on our credit cards or through bank loans the more we increase consumer debt. However, speculative debt is something else entirely and is by far the larger of the two, debt as a consequence of speculative investments such as stocks and shares, property investments and the like. Consumer debt has not had much impact on the worldwide banking crisis of 2008 onwards whereas speculative debt certainly has; take subprime mortgages for example where families on very low incomes were offered mortgages with no real prospect of paying them back resulting in record numbers of bank repossessions and the collapse of vast financial empires.

There is absolutely nothing wrong with wanting to own one's own home or acquire luxury, but the fact that we are bombarded through the media with images of the perfect life and all its accoutrements, it is often difficult to remain patient when time seems against you and that we, especially as men, cannot be the provider of all things. I try to think about this in terms of the 'concern/reward' equation. We must show a certain degree of concern in order to take the necessary action to improve and reward ourselves through the realisation of our ambitions. However too much concern can be as damaging as it invariably leads to the cancer of all ambitions, that of worry. Worry is a completely destructive behaviour that creates only more anguish and misery than it avoids. It is a debilitating condition and we should not allow ourselves the luxury of wallowing in it for just as we allow ourselves to be discouraged or not, we also allow ourselves to worry or not. Concern is a positive and healthy state that leads us to take affirmative action, whereas worry is completely counterproductive and only leads to apathy and resignation.

So, be concerned about your finances, by all means, but try not to allow yourself to become worried. If you decide that things will, and have to improve, then you have already taken the first bold step towards wanting them to improve. This invariably leads you to take the necessary action and therefore puts you a giant stride closer to realising your ambitions.

2.26 Being still and quiet.

"Stillness is the first requirement for manifesting your desires, because in stillness lies your connection to the field of pure potentiality that can orchestrate an infinity of details for you." Deepak Chopra.

To maintain an emotional balance is one of the most difficult tasks that require both self-analysis and constant vigilance. Self-analysis is often the most painful of all processes in that it means we must give ourselves up to a kind of internal psychotherapy. The best way to do this is to take time out with your Guru and get them to delve deeply into the fundamental aspects of our lives. To do this we must first be still and quiet in order to be both relaxed and open. (See sections 1.36 and 1.37 – Relaxation and meditation).

First of all, make sure you are relaxed and more importantly, open to the suggestions that your Guru may raise. Ask yourself some basic questions such as "Am I happy?" and "What areas of my life need improving?" "Do I have a good emotional balance?" and "How can I improve my emotional expression?" It may even help you if you ask these questions out loud whilst looking in the mirror. This may sound extremely basic but your subconscious, being the child it is, can only handle simplistic questions as your higher reasoning capacities lie elsewhere in what Deepak Chopra calls 'the field of pure potentiality'. This is literally the place where everything and anything is possible, a place where all things begin and where all things are created.

Previously we have looked at the benefits of meditation on stress reduction, however, the principles here on the benefits of being still and quiet, are not merely relaxation techniques. They are techniques with the specific objective of balancing our own energies with that of all the other energies in the universe and that when we are able to do that our overall well-being benefits which directly impacts on our emotional balance.

To illustrate the point let us consider times in our lives when we are constantly running around taking care of the business of our day to day lives. Where, from the moment we wake up, to the moment we go to sleep our lives are filled with something. We therefore, by definition, have something missing and that something is the essence of 'nothingness'. A time and a place where everything in our lives is put on hold while we recharge and refocus our intentions. Obviously the best method to do this is through meditation but it is thankfully not the only way to reach this state. Simply going out for a walk and sitting under a tree and just listening to the sounds around us can enable us to tune in to the ebb and flow of the universe. Or just by taking the phone off the hook and sitting in a quiet room we can then allow ourselves the time to feel the essence of stillness and therefore to collect our thoughts.

In his book 'The Seven Spiritual Laws of Success' Deepak Chopra states that when we actively engage in silence we must periodically withdraw from all other activities such as speech, watching TV, listening to the radio, or even reading. He also says that by not giving yourself the opportunity to experience silence creates turbulence in your internal dialogue. I have also found that when we do allow ourselves to be still and quiet we come to realise that our internal dialogue is virtually in constant flow. We tend not to realise when we lead a busy life that if we don't actively listen to this dialogue then we may actually miss something important. Maybe our Guru is telling us something of fundamental importance but because we have got to pick the kids up from school or get to the bank before it closes etc. we will miss out on what is being said. I visualise my Guru as resigning to sitting down, putting his feet up and reading the newspaper, stating "Well if you're not going to listen then why should I bother!" and the longer we don't listen the less he works for us.

2.27 Sex

> *"Too chaste an adolescence makes for a dissolute old age."*
> Andre Gide.

For me, and countless others, sex is one of the ultimate forms of emotional expression and as such requires subsequent examination as to why it is not only so important to us, but has also been throughout all of our civilised history. For countless centuries the lover in us has been celebrated as being a fundamental expression of our 'lust for life'. Beyond the mere act of species procreation, sex has also been described as the source of our spirituality, in that it encompasses the 'Oneness' of man and woman with the oneness of all that is.

Given the historical significance of this aspect of human behaviour it would be impossible not to consider how previous generations have interpreted sex in order for us to reach a greater understanding at this point in time. The Romans used to call it *amor*, the complete union of one body and soul with another. The Latin term *libido* actually means not just ones sexual appetite but also ones general appetite for life. The lover is seen as possessing a primal energy that we can also call passion, alertness and vividness and ultimately gives rise (excuse the pun!) to a greater meaning in life that human beings need in order to continue. This internal energy is inextricably linked to the energy sensitivity of the outer environment. Jungian psychologists use the term 'sensation function' as a function designed so that we can experience all of our sensory experiences, from sound and sight to tactile sensations such as smell and touch and the deep physiological effects that these create.

This is why we want to touch and to be touched for the aesthetic qualities that it brings. We all have a primal urge to be interconnected, not just with our lovers, but with all things where we can experience the poignancy of the world with all its pleasures and pains. However, more recently, the act of sex has also seemed to have been frowned upon as something dirty or even evil, so why is this? This stems from various religious and cultural influences. For instance Christianity, Judaism and Islam, which purport to be moral or ethical religions, have all tried to subdue these urges by various means. Christianity almost extensively teaches that the world, which is the very object of the aesthetics devotion, is evil and that the Devil is considered as the 'lord of the world' thereby being the source of all sensuous pleasures (sex being at the top) and is therefore something to be avoided at all costs (other than for procreation, not recreation). In Islam too women have been considered as second class (if they are lucky!) and consequently depreciated and even oppressed as they are considered as 'defilers' and a constant distraction to pious and 'righteous' men.

However, because sex is such a powerful emotion it has to be tempered in order for it not to become the one and only driving force in our lives. Sexual addicts are more common than you would recognise and as with any other addiction, the effects are usually devastating to their (and others) lives. The addicted lover asks: "Why should I limit myself to one person when the world is so filled with pleasures?" As with others with addictive personalities, such as eating too much, or drinking, or smoking, or doing drugs, their lives are never truly fulfilled as their cravings are never really satisfied. They move from one fix to the next, always in search of the ultimate high, or orgasm, or whatever. When it comes to sex we see what is known as the 'Don Juan Syndrome' where a man, or woman, moves from one partner to the next and by compulsively searching (for they know not what) and become (or have always been) a person who is non-centred. They are pushed and pulled around by one illusory experience to the next in the form of sexual experiences and the world presents itself as fragmented as they are fragmented from within. Could this be one of the reasons why there are so many absent fathers in the world today as they live out this image of moving from town to town in a never ending search for the perfect partner? But when the sex stops and the conversations begin and they find another imperfect human being they are seen riding off into the sunset in search of more (mis)adventures?

Conversely monogamy can be considered as an expression of deep-rootedness and a reflection of one's inner calm in that when you are comfortable with yourself you can then become comfortable with being with just one person without requiring the ego boost of somebody else saying how good you are. Also because sex with other people, particularly when you are in a stable or long-term relationship, can conjure up such powerfully destructive emotions such as jealousy and anger, this can, and has unfortunately on countless occasions, lead to much pain and even death by foul means. You catch a tiger by the tail if you underestimate the powerful forces that sex and the absence of sex can unleash.

It is worth mentioning here that if you feel as though you are suffering from a sex related issue such as not having satisfying sex or losing your sexual appetite or even needing too much sex then my advice would be to do something about it rather than letting the problem become even worse. As sex is so inextricably linked to so many other aspects of our emotional balance, such as a secure and happy relationship as well as self-esteem issues to name but a couple of examples, it is not going to do you (or your partner) any good if you ignore the issue and hope it will just go away. Talk to someone, get some advice, be proactive and enjoy your sex life because surely that's what it's all about, isn't it?

2.28 Sleep

"True silence is the rest of the mind; it is to the spirit what sleep is to the body, nourishment and refreshment." William Penn.

If there is one basic need that can disrupt our equilibrium more than any other it must surely be the lack of sleep. One can go without sex for prolonged periods of time and feel nothing more than a little grumpy. We can certainly go without being still and quiet without any debilitating effects. But to lose sleep for more than a day our bodies simply crash. Sleep is the ultimate in primordial necessity and a must for every single human being on the planet. It is both refreshing and luxurious and satisfies our physiological need to rejuvenate as well as our needs for warmth and comfort and, to many, the long lie-in is considered as much of a luxury as a well-earned holiday.

To consolidate this point we only have to look at the use of sleep deprivation for the use in interrogation where detainees are kept awake for long periods of time then interviewed over and over again in order to weaken their resolve and therefore are more likely to 'spill the beans'. Much research has taken place over the years about the effects of depriving people from sleep and then testing them using a variety of different models to assess their overall performance. Tests include patients driving in simulators, which invariably lead to crashes and accidents after relatively short periods of time. Tests also include mental dexterity questions, as well as getting the volunteers to build fairly basic structures with Lego or Sticklebricks that children could easily perform but sleep deprived adults cannot.

Once more much has been written on the subject of sleep and sleep deprivation and I only intend to add a smattering of information on the subject merely to underline its importance in maintaining our emotional equilibrium. Without resorting to the extremes of deliberate deprivation I want to consider the insidious effects of casually depriving oneself of sleep due to hectic schedules and working long hours. When you look back at times in your life when you have not had enough sleep ask yourself how did you feel and what effect this had on your emotional balance? Often, without the correct amount of sleep (which inevitably is different from person to person), you feel sluggish and not firing on all cylinders. Your concentration levels are impaired and your irritability is increased in direct proportion to the amount of sleep lost. You are less able to cope given a trying situation if you are sleep deprived than if you have had enough sleep. Consequently your emotional reactions are also impaired. What you could and would normally brush off as being unimportant takes on a new and seemingly insurmountable dimension where it seems to take nothing at all before you are in floods of tears, or very irritable where you will snap at the merest of provocation. Sound familiar?

However, as with all other polar extremes of behaviour, too much is often as bad as too little. Although we all enjoy sleeping and often wish that we could stay in our nice warm beds for a little bit longer, when we indulge in too much sleep our senses seem to be as dulled than if we have had no sleep at all. It becomes a vicious cycle, we sleep more and the more we sleep the more tired we feel and therefore require even more sleep.

Sleep is an odd conundrum, at one extreme it is completely necessary for us to function and at the other a seemingly huge waste of our valuable time. If we sleep eight hours a day and live to become seventy-five years old we have been asleep for over twenty-five years of our lives! This seems so vast that it underlines the importance of sleep on our biological functions, it is simply a must do and therefore a conscious juggling act to put enough time aside for this essential function as well as leaving enough time for us to live our lives to the fullest. There are no prescriptive formulas to be given regarding how much sleep each individual needs, some people seem to be able to get by on only a few hours per night, whilst others cannot function without at least eight hours or more. It is a juggling act that we learn throughout our lives and varies with many different external factors. If we have been working long and hard hours conducting extremely physical work, such as labouring, then we need more sleep than if we had been performing a more sedentary occupation. Also, if we are ill our bodies somehow tell us to rest, this goes for if we are both physically incapacitated or emotionally challenged. Think about it, when we are upset, for whatever reason, let's take heartbreak for example, we seem to gain a great deal of comfort by sleeping to block out the pain, don't we?

Sleep is like a medicine, but like all medicines it has to be regulated in order to gain the maximum effect. There's no point in taking all of your medicine at once and believing that it will do you much good. There's no point in doing the maths and working out that you need say fifty hours sleep a week and then simply sleeping for two days a week. The human biological function is a far too sophisticated machine to be maltreated in such a blatant way as this. Again it is the result of hundreds of thousands of years of evolution and to better understand its need we have to gain a fuller understanding of why it has developed as such an essential aspect in our lives. Let's face it; evolution does not do things by accident, only by design. We have been designed to sleep at night and be wakeful during the day. Human beings are not naturally nocturnal creatures and it is not remarkable to realise that the growing amount of sleep disorders are completely a modern phenomenon and part of the electric light bulb generation. Even a hundred years ago most people did not spend much waking time during the hours of darkness; they simply went to bed earlier and rose earlier the next day. (Have you ever noticed how so many of the 'older' or elderly generation still manage to be 'up with the lark'?) Also certain aspects of Traditional Chinese Medicine concentrate on doing just this by claiming that our bodies are out of sync if we continually and habitually stay awake during the hours of darkness. In fact they go further and proclaim that its long-term effects can be extremely devastating to our health.

But what if you live in a part of the world where it stays dark for many hours during the winter? Surely you can't be expected to go to bed at five-o-clock during the winter months? Obviously I am not suggesting this course of action at all. What I am suggesting is the essence of moderation. To be aware of when it is appropriate to sleep more and when it is inappropriate to sleep less. There are no formulas to be offered other than, once more, to listen to the wisdom of your inner Guru. You know better than anyone does how much sleep you need and how much sleeplessness you can get away with and over what periods of time.

2.29 Time with family

"Govern a family as you would cook small fish." Chinese proverb.

We have already touched on the importance of 'communing with our fellow man' in the section Time to Talk (2.17) in terms of our emotional expression. However, it would be wrong not to look more closely at how this impacts our emotional balance as the two are inextricably linked. We already, hopefully, understand the importance of man as a social creature, as to be devoid of company is to lessen the quality of our existences (Human Givens – Connection/Community). Therefore, we have to make deliberate and concerted efforts in our lives to make sure that we put enough time aside (and are allowed to) in our hectic lives to, not only enjoy our time with our families, but to view this precious time with as much necessity as sleep, drink, food and the very air that we breathe.

As an example I would like to discuss an extremely personal aspect in my life and how this creates, and gives me, a greater sense of balance and that is the time that I get to spend with my children. For me, and for countless other fathers, the very act of spending time with my kids has to be a deliberate act as I was separated from their mother when the children were very young and living miles apart we have to orchestrate every visit with almost military precision. This makes it sound as though our time together is clinical and cold but this is certainly not the case. The time I spend with my children is probably the most rewarding time that I get to spend with anyone else as I suppose the absence of their company on a day-to-day basis tends to turn each visit into a special occasion of its own.

I remember, in the early days after our separation, I found it emotionally very difficult and when I had said my goodbye's tears would often follow when driving away. Also, if more than a couple of weeks went by without me seeing them, I would experience an immense sense of incompleteness that could only be satiated by time with my kids. Fortunately, and I thank my Karma as well as my ex-partners reasonableness and understanding that a fathers input in the rearing of his children is as of much importance as the mothers, that we have had an amicable arrangement when it has come to seeing my kids. My heart bleeds for those fathers who have been denied access to their children, particularly through the outdated Family Court System, and cannot begin to imagine the devastating effects that this must have on their and their children's emotional equilibrium.

I recently watched a TV programme about the group 'Fathers 4 Justice' and their plights and exploits regarding the issue of fathers being denied access to their children and without exception saw that their emotional centres were far from aligned, resulting in all manner of desperate actions and attitudes. Simply put, if these fathers were allowed time with their children their emotional balance would be far more complete than their current situations. We are genetically programmed to spend time with those that we love in as much as the duckling is hard wired to accepting that the first thing it sees when it comes out of the shell is its mother. We have a very basic (not just) human need to be with our families and to share our lives and experiences. For me, as the years went by, I found it a lot easier to say goodbye knowing that it wouldn't be long before I saw my kids again. I can't imagine the agony of those that when they say goodbye don't know if they will see their kids again, never mind when.

I also believe that this enforced separation that is being inflicted on countless fathers is not only detrimental to themselves and their children but also to society at large. A staggering fifteen billion pounds per year is spent in the UK alone dealing with the effects of marital breakdowns. Something like eighty percent of all social welfare housing is for single-parent families and statistics show that a child from a one-parent family is five times more likely to be unemployed and three times more likely to go to prison than a child reared equally by both parents. The seeds that are being planted today are raising a desperate generation that in turn are planting the seeds of their own in unknown territory.

It is an undeniable fact that children today generally do not experience positive role models as much as previous generations. Millions of children are growing up without their fathers and therefore are simply ill equipped to define their own gender role models which, in time, will inevitably lead to their own future relationship problems (as well as social problems such as civil disorders etc.) Children, like all of us, only learn through direct experience and if that very experience is denied them they will grow into maladjusted adults, never really knowing what is right and what is wrong. What the essences of family love are all about and therefore miss out on its many tender splendours.

As previously discussed, we are tactile creatures who are meant to touch and be touched. We are built to cuddle and tickle and to laugh and read stories before bed-time and to deny ourselves these life essentials is ultimately to deny our own humanity. This can only lead to a downward spiral of discourse, bitterness, anger and hatred. The first line of the 1989 Children's Act states that: "Any actions taken, the best interests of the children are paramount." In this I agree. To deny a child access to becoming a fully rounded citizen should be of grave concern to us all as it, and is already, creating great divisions within our societies that may well be leading to the detrimental effects that are so evident in society today. When a child is deprived of love they can always learn hate and if they learn hate we had better all watch out! The increase in 'drive-by' shootings bears testament to this point as well as the recent disturbances on the streets of Britain. When you tamper with the fabric of family life, you tamper with the very fabric that holds society together.

For children, and fathers, rituals are important in the bonding process and the absence of these rituals leaves a huge gap in their lives. When I talk of rituals I am not talking about ancient initiation ceremonies or tests of manhood or the like, I am talking about the little rituals of eating together, bathing and cleaning, tucking up in bed and reading stories, of talking and laughing. Tests have shown that children who spend more time with their fathers are more likely to become well adjusted adults with securer long-term family relationships of their own as fractured families often lead to scarred children, frustrated parents and even distraught grandparents. It becomes an agonising series of events that inevitably leads to emotional imbalance. So, in order to maintain our own balance and that of our children, we must accept that children love both of their parents and that both of their parents love them and that time together is essential.

CONTROL

From the dictionary definition part of the description of control means *to regulate*. It is a common misconception that control of your emotions means to keep a lid on them and not to express them. This is wrong. You cannot control your emotions by not expressing them as they will invariably control you. To control here means to be in touch with your emotions and at the same time (once more) to have a balance between when it's right to express them and when it's wrong. To be aware of your feelings and at the same time to *regulate* them as to how you should express them appropriately or otherwise. Ultimately this depends on whether or not you express your emotions constructively or destructively.

More emotional problems will inevitably be caused if you try to restrain your feelings rather than let your feelings be known. You must put yourself in a position where you can find the balance between being in touch with your feelings and not letting them control you. A good analogy would be riding a horse. You must offer encouragement whilst at the same time keeping a good grip of the reins showing the horse, in a gentle but firm way, who is the boss. For as we know, if a horse feels it has control over you then you are bound to end up bruised!

To be in control of our emotions is all about balancing our emotional expression in the middle ground rather than the polar extremes. The middle ground here is obviously between completely controlling and bottling up our emotions and allowing our emotions to control us. We have already looked at the importance of emotional expression and balance as well as the damaging effects of not doing so. It is also equally important to not allow our emotions to control us. Think of the scorned lover who becomes the possessive stalker or the bereaved relative who becomes the killer, to mention just two examples of those under the control of their negative and destructive emotions.

This type of person is normally categorised as the person who cannot let go of the past and turns their feelings towards destruction (usually on themselves but often on others.) The past is the past and there is nothing that anybody who has ever lived can do about it, all we can do is to somehow reconcile what has taken place, learn to deal with our emotions in a positive way and then try to make the most out of the time we have left rather than allow events to rule and ruin our existence. In fact, a far more common sense thing to do is to attempt to somehow turn our misfortunes into benefits. The example of Colin and Wendy Parry specifically comes to mind who I have had the pleasure of working for at the Warrington Peace Centre.

For those unfamiliar with their story here is a brief background. In March 1993, on the day before Mothering Sunday, their twelve year old son Tim was in Warrington town centre, along with hundreds of other kids buying their mothers cards, flowers and chocolates. Just before midday an IRA bomb, which had been planted in a bin, exploded. Four year old Jonathan Ball was in his pushchair and took the full force of the blast dying instantly. Fifty-six other people were taken to hospital, some lost limbs. Tim was close to the bin-turned-grenade and was struck in the head by flying shrapnel. He never regained consciousness and five days later Colin and Wendy were forced to make the agonising decision to turn off his life-support machine. Tim died quietly in their arms but the Parry's lives would never be the same. Of all of life's traumas, losing a child in such a horrific way must be one of the worst imaginable. So what did they do? They could have done what any other parent could have done in their situation. They could have closed the curtains and dealt with their pain, grief and anger in private, but no, they decided to fight! To fight to make Tim's life mean something, and I don't mean getting out the guns and bullets and going to Northern Ireland to hunt down their son's killers. No, theirs was a hunt for a real kind of justice that can only be found in peace and reconciliation.

That awful day Colin and Wendy became peace activists. They decided to travel to Ireland, North and South and attempt to unravel the mystery of the reasons behind Tim's death. Considering the background of 'The Troubles' theirs was a gargantuan and Herculean task. However, their actions seemed to galvanise the nations and politicians on both sides of the border as well as across their embattled communities. Businessmen and royalty alike backed their cause and consequently they created The Peace Centre where young people from Belfast, Dublin and Warrington could share time and dialogue together to build bridges of peace between their divided communities. They have certainly succeeded in doing so and continue to do so to this day. (In fact Colin was later awarded the OBE for his efforts towards creating a long lasting peace.) The point that I am making is that, even given the terrible events of the past, they have been able to turn the poison of murder into the medicine of peace, they have turned a tragedy in their own lives into triumph in the lives of countless others and have undoubtedly played a major part in creating the comparative peace that Ireland now enjoys. Whereas they could have quite easily allowed their raw emotions to control them and turn them, as Darth Vader would say, 'to the dark side', to that of hatred and violence, but that was a choice that they were never prepared to make.

Emotional control is a constant balancing act between when and how to express ourselves. It is all about the choices *we* make as no one else gets to choose our emotional reactions but us. We may have little control of events and situations that elicit an emotional response but we do get the unique opportunity to do what enlightened human beings do best and that is to choose how to react. The situations may be the same but the outcomes are completely different, from inappropriate and destructive to appropriate and constructive.

2.31 The illusion of control

"The greatest happiness is to transform one's feelings into action."
Madame de Stael.

Of all of life's illusions the most prevalent must be that of control. The story of King Canute comes to mind where he was under the illusion that he could control everything, even the tides, by his rule of command, and we all know his fate, that of disaster. We have very little control over certain events in our lives, particularly accidents. We cannot control the seasons or any of the other physical laws of the universe as this is mere folly and symptomatic of mans arrogance. Human beings are adept at harnessing the power of nature, hydroelectric and wind power generated electricity are good examples, but, in the words of 'Scotty' in Star Trek *"You canny break the laws of physics."* Nor can we control the events of our lives completely. Yes, we have the choice of turning left instead of right and the choice of fight or flight, but this is where it ends. If we turn left and are run over by a bus then there is very little else that can be done. The one thing that we do have an element of control over is the reaction we have to events rather than the actual events themselves. Colin and Wendy Parry had zero control of the events on that fateful day but their reactions have ultimately been creative as opposed to destructive.

When all is said and done you are the only person responsible for your reactions, nobody else can dictate to you how to act or react, you decide. This is ultimately the only control that we truly have. So, for instance, if someone you had never met walked up to you and smacked you in the face your immediate reaction may be to hit them back but in doing so you would probably make the situation worse. You decide whether or not you walk away or retaliate, no one else. Similarly if you have experienced a distressful period in your life you get to decide how much and in what way that shapes your future. You may have had a succession of disastrous relationships and therefore decide that all men/women are all the same and the best thing to do is having nothing what so ever to do with them thereby denying yourself the opportunity of a long lasting loving relationship at any point in the future. Or you may have had a negative experience with someone from another place and then prejudice everyone else from that place as having the same characteristics. The point is you get to choose how much of this excess baggage you want to carry around with you for the rest of your lives. No one else makes the baggage heavier than you and you can rest assured that no one else will want to carry it for you either! So, the question has to be, why would you want to burden yourself with the events of the past? In doing so you will find that reaching your destination will be a lot more difficult, if not downright impossible!

You will never be able to reach the summit of a light future if you carry the heavy burden of the past.

Maybe I should have entitled this section 'The control of illusion' in that it is often our illusions (prejudices of ourselves as well as others) that control us. If we allow our illusions to control our thoughts then they will inevitably control our actions and therefore our eventual outcomes.

2.32 Working in unison

"The best and safest thing is to keep a balance in your life, acknowledge the great powers around us and in us. If you can do that, and live that way, you are really a wise man." Euripides.

As with most things in life we continually have to work to find the middle ground between two opposite ends of the spectrum, in this case between controlling our emotions and allowing our emotions to control us as neither one is an entirely healthy state to be in. However there are times in our lives, particularly when experiencing the grief of bereavement for example when it would be foolish (if not impossible) to control our emotions. When someone that we love, be it a family member, friend, someone (or something else as in the case of a close pet) we know or even a celebrity that we admire dies we are left, quite naturally, with a sense of overwhelming loss and it would be considered as completely inappropriate if we were not to show it. We have previously discussed how our emotions make us truly human it would therefore be completely inappropriate not to express our emotions during these most difficult of times. In actual fact research has shown that to bottle our emotions up at this time can be extremely damaging both physically, in terms of damaging our immune systems and causing illness, as well as psychologically.

I recently heard a radio programme talking about how we risk turning a perfectly normal reaction, e.g. sadness, into a condition to be treated. Specifically doctors are increasingly prescribing medications to people who are quite naturally going through the grieving process rather than allowing them to go through the process naturally. OK, if someone is suffering to such an extent that their sleep is continually being interrupted and they are prescribed sleeping tablets on a temporary basis, then fine. However people are being prescribed mind altering medications such as those being prescribed to individuals with varying degrees of mental illness, which to my mind is completely inappropriate. Sadness is not a sickness; it's a process that we naturally have to go through.

We are meant to grieve so why mask it? Likewise we are meant to express other emotions at certain times in our lives, it's just a matter of knowing which to express, when to express them and to what magnitude, including the length of time to express them for. Let's look at a fictional character as an extreme example of what not to do, the character of Miss Haversham in Dickens Great Expectations who had been grieving for over two decades after being spurned by her fiancé and left standing at the altar. Sure enough, if this were to happen it is only right and proper to feel less than great but Miss Faversham had allowed her grief to become so self-consuming that all she could do was to live her life as a total recluse and to plot her revenge against all men, believing that they are all the same and that they should all be punished. This resulted in her life being one of misery and despair, as well as creating misery and despair in the lives of others.

So when does a belief become an obsession and who is to say how much we should grieve and to what extent and for how long? Unfortunately there is no guide to this nor is there a set prescribed timescale. Once more it is a matter of using our Guru wisdom in order to get our answers. Considering the loss of a loved one we accept that to grieve is only right and proper but to allow it to destroy the rest of our lives is a formula for disaster and presumably not what our loved one would want us to do. However, in certain cases, it is absolutely amazing (and of course a testament to the resilience of the human spirit) how people can recover at all given the magnitude of some tragedies. At the time of writing this passage the world is being rocked by a series of devastating floods in Australia and South America claiming hundreds of lives. Some people lost whole families and I wonder how they are able to carry on at all when their whole lives have been changed irrevocably in an instant.

2.33 Retrospective

"Why do I do the things I don't want to; and the very things I want to do, I can't?" St Paul.

How many times have we said to ourselves "If only I had said this" or "If only I had done that"? Hindsight is a wonderful thing isn't it? It makes us re-evaluate the situations we find ourselves in, our reactions to the situations and their eventual outcomes. It also gives us the opportunity to replay the events as well as taking comfort in the fantasy of creating alternative outcomes. I am sure that at some point we have all looked back at an undesirable episode in our lives and wished that we had done something different. I recently heard the phrase 'Highway Lines', those things we wished we had said when we are driving away from an unpleasant situation. In some people however, the fantasy/illusion that has played over and over again in their minds becomes so strong a force that it deletes the actual event itself and the illusion or fantasy becomes the reality. This is not only a common trait amongst the mentally ill but also a mechanism to those who have suffered extreme trauma (the prisons are also full of people who have convinced themselves that they are completely innocent). The fabricated reality becoming the true reality is not however limited to people on the margins of society as it happens all the time with what could be considered as sound minded and rational people. One only has to watch the nightly news to see the way spin turns opinion into fact!

There is however some good news, the more we practice reflection the more we learn about ourselves and our appropriate place in the world. To put it another way, if we were not to reflect on our actions and outcomes then all of our social mores and graces would never have the chance to develop and we would quickly be marginalised and misaligned. Simply put, when we use our ability to be retrospective we improve, when we lose it or abuse it, we don't. To be retrospective means to be mindful of ourselves and our interactions with others and is an integral part of our emotional intelligence as well as our self improvement process as it makes us re-evaluate not just our actions but also our opinions, motivations and behaviours.

It is a bit like an addict admitting their addiction being the first step towards their eventual recovery. When we recognise that we have a problem we are a huge step closer to creating the solution. Conversely, if all we do is think and believe that we are always right and that we have no need to modify our behaviour, let alone reflect on the outcomes, then all we will ever do is sail through life from one storm to the next always believing that it's always the others guys fault or asking ourselves the eternal losers question "Why does this always happen to me?" When we look back and realise that we could have done better then the chances are that in the future we probably will. This is a lot like perspective; you either use it or lose it. Retrospective thought gives us the unique opportunity to make reparation from the past and improvement for the future. It is the very essence of our ability to learn. When we burn ourselves on the white hot metal of experience we know next time what not to touch. We forge our own future upon the anvil of the past.

Once more we must visit our Guru for this is the place where our reflection takes place. Our internal Guru watches everything and records it completely objectively. Our Guru will give us the best advice we could ever wish to receive, all we have to do is ask. As long as we trust the advice and accept the fact that we are still a work in progress then we will empower ourselves to deal with situations and circumstances a lot better in the future.

2.34 Perseverance

"Many strokes overthrow the tallest oaks." John Lyly.

The art of success is all about finding something that works and then doing it over and over again! It is the proverbial 1% inspiration and 99% perspiration. When you employ the ability of retrospection you then begin the process of getting closer to the eventual solution being more in your favour and the more you do this the better you get, it's as simple as that. Perseverance comes with our dedicated and continual actions. What makes a great athlete other than perseverance and dedication? What creates art, is it talent or application? There's no point in having a great idea and then doing nothing about it.

"Good luck is another name for tenacity of purpose."
Ralph Waldo Emerson.

I like this definition as it leaves a whole lot of room for our actions rather than luck being merely down to chance. Thomas Jefferson said; *I'm a great believer in luck and I find the harder I work, the more I have of it.* More often than not those people who have the ability to prepare themselves for success are usually more successful than those who merely wait for success to happen. Even lottery winners had to take the action of going out and buying a ticket living by the adage that 'you have to be in it to win it'. You will never win the race if you are either late for the start or you merely amble along when others are running as fast as they can.

Another adage comes to mind, 'those who fail to plan, plan to fail'. If you don't have a map how are you supposed to get to where you are going? There's no point in turning up at the airport and saying to the girl at check-in and saying "I'd like to go somewhere hot please?" and not expect for her to look at you as if you have lost your mind. Apart from merely making a vague plan our plans must contain as much detail as possible. We are then in a position to be able to follow this plan through to the letter and how good does it feel when we have put a tick next to every single action point on a list? Sometimes there is no need for praise from others when our own self congratulations are reward enough.

Perseverance is all about making a plan and then sticking to it no matter what happens. It is all about making determinations like 'I will get fitter' or 'I will pass those exams' or 'I am going to make a success of this venture no matter how much my friends and family may laugh behind my back'. It's all about rising above the opinions of others and applying oneself as if one's life depends upon it. It's all about having sufficient self esteem to motivate oneself into working long and hard towards fulfilling your ambitions and creating balance and contentment. It's also all about overcoming difficulties and obstacles, making necessary sacrifices and completing what you set out to do. Perseverance is not for quitters it is for those who are prepared to go the extra mile and pull out all the stops in order to achieve their objectives.

2.35 Irritability/annoyance

"We are not going to deal with the violence in our communities, our homes, and our nation, until we learn to deal with the basic ethic of how we resolve our disputes and to place an emphasis on peace in the way we relate to one another." Marian Wright Edelman.

For those who suffer from the condition of irritability or annoyance your future bywords must become 'retrospect' and 'persevere'. You have to consult your Guru and learn the dual abilities of observing your behaviour as to the triggers of your annoyance and to persevere to creating a more appropriate means of expression until you have finally broken the habit, which, when all is said and done, is all it is, a habit and like any habit, it can be broken.

Irritability is a bit like being overweight. First of all it's not good for you (as well as those around you) and second, you hold the solution within your own willpower. Like any bad habit you have over the years allowed it to become part of your make up to the extent that you are probably unaware that you are doing it until somebody else points it out to you. Fortunately though, like any other bad habit, it can be broken. All you have to do is realise that you are suffering from this condition and decide to do something about it. When the addict finally says 'I'm an addict' they have taken their first steps towards their eventual recovery.

First of all, when looking at any addiction, you must look at the payoff. What's in it for you to keep on repeating this form of negative expression? Why do you allow yourself to lose your cool or is it always 'somebody else's fault'? Let's face it one more time, no one else can dictate your irritability or annoyance only you can. Okay, external circumstances can play their part in whether or not you display this behaviour but (yet again) your reaction is entirely under your control and no one else's. So, what you have to do is to analyse the payoff and in doing so you will get a huge step closer to realising that it does no one any good what-so-ever. By doing this you will probably find that you have, more often than not, always behaved in such a manner in order to get your way. When you become annoyed it's usually because things are not going the way you planned or you are not getting your way. Take for example road rage where people will become completely irrationally enraged just because someone has cut them up or because they are late for an appointment. Irritability has turned beyond annoyance into anger, then into out and out rage, where people have actually killed, or even been killed.

These are extreme cases but on the whole these negative expressions seem to be more prevalent today than they have ever been, so why is this? Is it because our own individual sense of importance is so inflated that it doesn't matter how rude or aggressive we are to others? Are we so important that others become less so? Or is it that we are simply like children that have never been told what is right and what is wrong and therefore allowed to behave in such an antisocial manner?

From my experience as a youth worker I have seen too many times the complete and utter lack of parental responsibility and control which results in young people growing up without boundaries and believing that anything goes.

For those that are still clinging to this misguided view of themselves and the world there is only one thing to say to a child who is yet to mature; grow up and start taking responsibility for your actions! Stop blaming others and take control of your negative expressions. You may not have had the best upbringing where you have been allowed to vent your frustrations in this manner but that was then and this is now! Stop clinging onto a misguided view of the past and live up to your realisation of the future. Ultimately, if you want others to respond to you positively then you must adopt a more positive approach to every situation that you encounter. You must also learn to become your own internal parent and by doing so you can look at your actions and reactions and decide if they have been right or wrong and if they have been wrong you must learn to discipline yourself and modify your response next time.

For instance, when you find yourself in a stressful situation where your gall is rising and your irritability and annoyance are beginning to surface remind yourself of two things. One; that you recognise what is happening, and two; to say to yourself that you will not allow yourself to lose your cool. Consequently your reaction will not only be different this time around but also next time you recognise when it's happening you will be better able to control your reactions and ultimately your own self actualised outcomes. These are the basic techniques that are used in any form of self appraisal and anger management, to recognise the triggers and then to decide to react in a completely different way, it really is that simple. Don't be a slave to your feelings, you must master your reactions in order to change your actions to affect your outcomes and in doing so you need never suffer (and the people around you need never suffer) from this debilitating and self deprecating condition ever again.

Annoyance and irritability are also an expression of the deepest disrespect, not just of others, but also of yourself. If you hold the basic premise that, not only are people basically good but more than that; that there is a spark of the divine (see Spirituality later) in every single person (if you possess an internalised Guru then it also stands to reason that everyone else also has this potentiality) and because of that they deserve fundamental respect. However, some people may not always manifest their Guru nature. Either they are not aware of it, or it simply might not be working for them that day and you happen to have interacted with them at the wrong time. Either way they still deserve respect. Consequently, if you deny someone else's Guru nature, you deny your own. If you disrespect someone, you disrespect yourself. If you use harsh words, you wound. Words can indeed be sharper than knives!

2.36 A few techniques

"Purpose is so that people can become more aware so that they can think more clearly and live their lives more effectively and efficiently."
Anon.

Goal setting is the lifeblood of all training and coaching for without a goal in mind how are you ever going to tell if you have scored? Without a target how will you know what to aim at? However, some people set themselves the trap of setting too higher goals in too shorter timescale thereby setting themselves up for a fall even before they have begun. I see it in my local gymnasium and swimming pool every January where good intentioned people say to themselves 'this year I'm going to get myself fit'. So they enrol in every class and buy all of the latest designer workout gear and leap into their unrealistic training schedule like persons possessed. But what happens? They are so stiff after a couple of classes that they give it up altogether. (How many discarded stepping, rowing and sit-up machines litter the garages of our land?)

The best way to get the best results is to use a tried and tested formula and then stick to it. The formula I propose is what is known as SMART objectives.

S means **Specific**. Your goals cannot be vague or woolly they must be exact. To use the holiday metaphor once more, there is no point in rewarding yourself with a vague promise of some kind of break wherever and at some point in the future. No, you must be able to say to yourself 'here is where I am going to go'.

M means **Measurable**. i.e. there must be some way of quantifying your goal so, if you are writing a book for instance, you must be able to put down an actual target of the amount of words per day/week/month that you want to achieve as an absolute minimum and that any more should be considered as a bonus.

A stands for **Achievable**. Your goals should not be too high as to be consistently unachievable nor set too low to become unchallenging. Graduate your goals by starting with goals that you consider easily achievable and then week on week increase to the point of realistic expectations.

R is **Realistic**. There is no point wanting to become a successful runner and then setting yourself the goal of being the first person to run a three minute mile! When you set your goals in reality they have a far better chance of becoming so.

T stands for **Timed**. Every goal must have a realistic and achievable timescale. If you are new to a sport it would be unrealistic to become world champion after a matter of weeks when others have taken years to master it. That's not to say that you shouldn't aim high but to aim for an achievable goal is far more realistic than setting yourself up to fail.

Spider Diagram

Here's a little, but fascinating exercise for you. Take a pen and paper and draw a large circle. Now draw a line from top to bottom and side to side, making four equal segments. Now draw two more lines from 'corner to corner' i.e. making eight equal wedges. (See diagram) Now, simply mark each line 1 – 8.

At this point I want you to take a little time aside to write down a list of the most important things in your life. The things that make you the happiest and most fulfilled. The things that give you that sense of balance and contentment where you know that as you fulfil all of these things on your list you are truly at peace with yourself. These might include, but certainly are not limited to, spending time with your loved ones, your career, your creativity, exercise, fun etc.

Now – choose your top eight. This sounds easier than it is as you should hopefully have quite a long list, but here's a simple tip. Put the thing that you couldn't live without at the very top. Then put the very next thing second. Before long you will be down to the last couple of choices, and these are always the hardest, so take your time discarding those last couple of things that you know, if push came to shove you could actually live without until you are eventually comfortable with your top eight (bearing in mind that this may also change over time) but this is your top eight of today, so date it. Write down the date you do this at the top of the page (for future reference – I recently came across one that I had done for myself eight years ago and it made very interesting reading!)

Here's what to do. Zero is the point where all the lines meet in the centre. 100% is the other end of the line that bisects the circle. Now I want you to score yourself from one to one hundred how much effort, time, emphasis you are putting into that important aspect of your life. So for instance, you might have health or exercise as one of your points. (I hope so – if not read section 1, Physical) If you are at your very best put a mark at 100%, but if you are honest with yourself (which is an essential aspect of this process as no one else is going to have to see your score) it may well be less. So put your mark where it really is, today, right now.

Figure 7 : Your Top 8

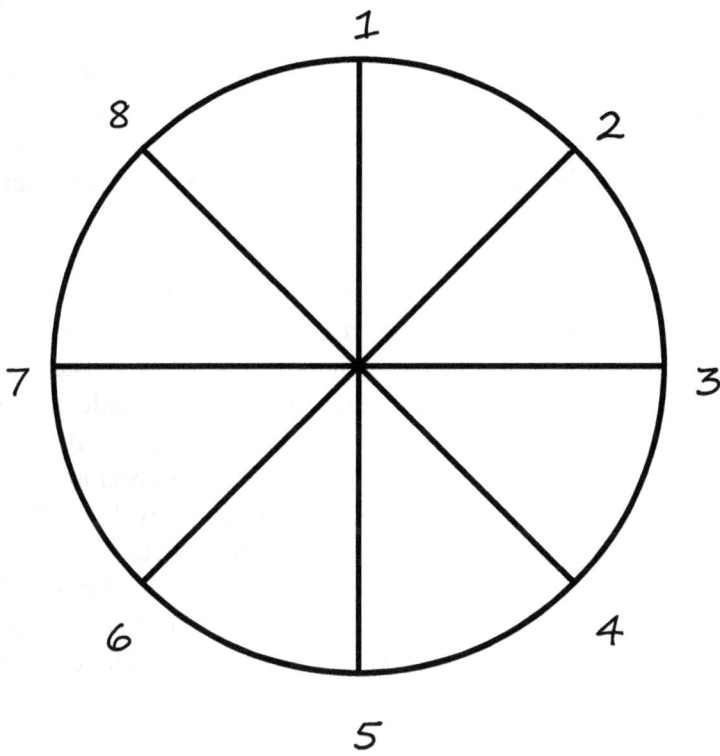

Then repeat this process for the remaining seven. Once you have eight marks join them up, like a dot-to-dot, this will result in your spider diagram. Hopefully it will show you those areas in your life that you have somehow neglected. Time with family and friends may be important to you, but for the proverbial 'one reason and another' you have not had enough time for them recently – so make time. It's what gives you fulfilment, enjoyment and balance. It's important, so make time. You may have creativity, or business or fun and adventure on your list but, as John Lennon so eloquently put it *"Life is what happens*

to you when you're busy making other plans" you may not have had the time to fulfil these aspects so (you know what I'm going to say) MAKE TIME!

These are the things that are most important to you, these are the things that define your very existence, the things that make you who you are and when you are fulfilling all of these things you become the best possible you, and what better way to be in the world! The world seems a better place, and you make it so. You become a person who others naturally gravitate to, you have resonance. So not only do you owe it to yourself, you owe it to the world to be content, at peace with yourself and in complete balance with your internal and external worlds.

Okay, so what have you got to look forward to once you have emotional stability in your life? It is important to realise what achieving your goals will do to enhance your life and daily existence. Once you have emotional stability you can really start to build a future full of hope and free from anxiety where any challenging situation you find yourself in can easily be dealt with and what previously seemed like insurmountable obstacles will now seem like a walk in the park. Your self-esteem improves in direct proportion to your sense of worth and value. Your opinions and suggestions will hold the weight and the authority of wisdom. This comes down to the basic premise of self-respect, for without this it is virtually impossible to command the respect of others.

When you combine self-respect with your new found physical prowess that you will gain from also working on your physical centre you will find yourself somehow walking taller, you will have greater self-confidence and no longer be reliant on the opinion of others. History has shown that all the great human beings have possessed this most valuable of commodities, to rise above the opinion of others, because, let's face it, that's all it is, an opinion. It is not a final judgement it is merely an opinion and probably from someone who has got their own emotional instabilities to deal with.

However, there is another aspect of your life that will augment this new found confidence and that is the mysterious and wondrous nature of your spirituality.

PART 3

SPIRITUAL

We have looked in detail how to create balance within ourselves physically and emotionally. We will now explore probably the most fascinating aspects of what arguably makes us truly human. The aspect that truly separates us from all other creatures on Earth. That thing which raises us above the mundane and commonplace; our spiritual capacities. Man is far more than a walking biped with opposable thumbs and the ability to make and utilise tools, if this were so we would still be living the same existences as our ancient ancestors. We are also more than our abilities to express ourselves emotionally as we possess the uniquely human characteristic of the ability to question.

When we ask 'why' or 'how' or 'what' then we are truly beginning to express ourselves as fully rounded human beings. There are no other species on Earth that has the ability to ask the questions "Why are we alive?" and "How does this work?" and "What is life really all about?" We, as human beings, have that unique burning desire to need to know the answers to these, and many other questions, to give our lives a deeper sense of meaning otherwise life would merely be an exercise in survival. All we would do is occupy our time with the tasks of providing food, warmth and shelter and all of the other basic requirements of just living.

Most of us have at some time or other in our lives realised that when we are working hard with no breaks and very little time for fun and relaxation and recreation, we ask ourselves that age old question, "There has to be more than this?" So, what is this 'more' and why do we feel as though we need to find it? Why do we ponder our very existences and why do we yearn for a greater purpose?

The three aspects of maintaining spiritual balance are:

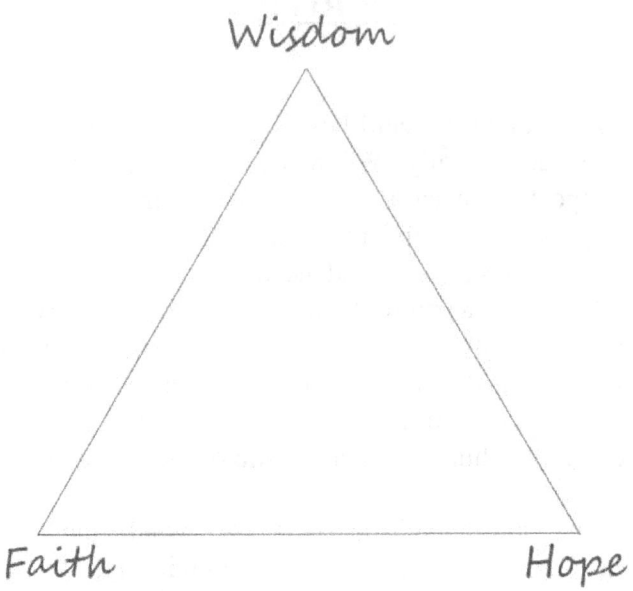

Figure 8: Spiritual Balance

In the Wisdom section we will discuss keeping moving forward no matter what challenges we face and how to focus on creating a higher purpose in our lives. We will also consider what it means to be truly happy and self-empowered.

The section on Faith explores what is means to have a faith, finding a faith and how faith empowers us as opposed to how it may disempower us. We will also discuss the pit falls of blind faith and how to awaken our own Guru nature.

Finally Hope deals with keeping our eye on the prize and considers the difference between merely believing and really knowing. Ultimately we will look at what action we need to take and how to trust in Guru-U.

WISDOM

The evolution of our species is a continual process of development and improvement. Homo sapiens may possess many admirable qualities but it is by no means the end of our evolutionary process. It is just another step in the direction of improvement. Many others beside me firmly believe that we are at the dawn of a new development of our species from Homo Sapiens to 'Homo Sentient' or 'thinking man' where we will utilise our brains capacity to a far greater extent than we do currently. History has shown us how great a contradiction Homo Sapiens are. We possess the abilities of appreciation whilst at the same time are destructive. We place value on trust and friendship whilst we are capable of betrayal. We all long for peace and security yet still wage war on our fellow man. Consequently we are still a long way from fully realising our potentials, both in microcosm and macrocosm.

Scientific progress has led to many great discoveries and yet still we cannot answer the basic questions of existence, like where did we come from? Why are we here? Where are we headed? In the twentieth century alone the joint disciplines of Cosmology and quantum physics have pondered and researched these very questions in finite detail and are still no closer to finding the holy grail of all theories, the so-called unified theory, or as Albert Einstein put it, 'The Theory of Everything'. One thing that now seems beyond reasonable doubt is that all life originates from a single source, The Big Bang. Every single particle in our bodies, as well as the planet on which we live (and the solar system and countless galaxies) all originate from that single moment in time some 13.7 billion years ago.

We are all children of the Universe and consequently share a common heritage. Effectively we are all one and the same. Our basic needs for food, warmth and shelter are the same whether we live in the city or the country or whether we live in the ice or the tropics. Also our basic human desires are also the same, as in our need for love, peace and harmony (see Human Givens.) We also share a common heritage in our varying degrees of spirituality otherwise the important questions that occupy us would not keep reoccurring.

When physicists analysed the content of matter they have discovered that there was actually more space between the component parts of atoms than there were actual components and that the primary difference between one substance and another is merely a vibrational quality. In the beginning there was only one basic element, hydrogen. As these atoms merged together (as the urge of all life and its ruling principle is to move together to form a more complex and higher state) denser pockets were formed which in turn excited these molecules to produce heat. These pockets fused together and leapt to the next level of vibration and created the element we now know as helium. As the process repeated itself over and over again all of the building blocks of life were created, next came lithium, which vibrated at the next highest level and so on and so on and so on, producing what is now known as The Periodic Table of Elements.

Eventually the element of carbon was formed and the next phases of our evolution really kick started. As our sun formed pockets of matter and fell into orbit around it one of them contained such a massive diversity of all of these elements that the Earth was created in a molten cauldron. As the Earth cooled gases that were once caught in the molten mass moved to the surface and created the first water vapours which in turn cooled the Earth creating its crust. Pools of water formed creating the oceans and in the shallower pools, charged by lightning storms that ravaged the Earth, a form of matter was created that existed on a higher vibrational level even than carbon, what we now know as the amino acids.

The strange thing about these substances was that they were not stable by themselves and required the continual consumption of other matter in order to maintain this higher vibrational state; in short they had to eat! A new era in evolution had begun and this new era took on three very distinct forms, the organic, in organic and the animal. Plants evolved by living on consuming inorganic matter such as absorbing carbon dioxide and producing oxygen. Animals in turn survived by consuming organic matter, branching off from aquatic to amphibious and eventually into land dwelling creatures. Each subsequent evolution that emerged moved into a higher and higher vibrational complexity ending with the ultimate progression of humankind. Human beings are the pinnacle of evolutionary advancement which has as its sole intention to move us and the whole universe into an even higher state of complexity. What we now have to ask ourselves is does evolution merely stop with us as its ultimate expression or is it meant to carry on as it always has? If we accept that we are meant to progress and that we do indeed already operate at a higher vibrational level then we must embrace the fact that we are indeed special, unique, and even divine.

The nature and magnitude of our spiritual quest lies at the root of this whole concept. Do we accept that a higher form of energy exists and that we are indeed an embodiment of that higher vibrational force and if so what are we going to do about it? If we are either already aware that this is true or willing to suspend our disbelief that this may be so, or even have an intuition that this is so without a satisfactory explanation or empirical proof then we can only do one of two things about it. We either accept it as truth or we do not. If we do not accept that we are part of a higher state of existence then there is more that you still have to learn which I am unable to explain you here and now.

However, if you do accept this as truth then I will return to my basic premise, what are you doing about it? Again you have two choices, to deliberately find a way of expanding this energy through actual practice, or simply ignore it all together and quit before you have even begun! The choices are that clear, choose to do it or choose not to! But if you decide that you do not wish to move to a higher vibrational complexity and live a life of higher purpose and meaning all I can do is ask WHY?

Why would you choose to deliberately hold yourself back from developing yourself? Would you prefer to remain closer to your hunter/gatherer existence or to evolve into something higher? As evolution does not reverse the only way we can go is forward and deliberately choosing not to progress is not only the mark of the ignorant it is also the mark of the arrogant and the foolish. You are meant to progress. You are meant to move forward. You are meant to be at the cutting edge of not only a new species but also a new civilization.

From Mans earliest origins we have pondered the laws of nature that govern us. The most ancient civilisations would worship the sun or the moon. They would build monuments such as stone circles which have now been attributed to marking the path of the suns orbit in the sky dictating the seasons and recognition that there are other forces at play above and beyond our everyday lives and that we are somehow and inextricably connected to them. Some theories, such as the renowned scientist Terrance McKenna in his theory entitled 'The Stoned Ape', expound that mans spiritual awareness became awakened as we discovered psycho active substances where we became 'aroused' on three specific levels; the first being that of visually stimulated where our visual acuity becomes enhanced, which is extremely good news if we rely on hunting. Some would argue, that those tribes that utilised substances such as psilocybin that are found in some mushrooms, were in fact the most successful in that they were able to catch a lot more food. The second level of arousal is actual physical arousal, literally, as it sounds, we became more sexually aroused and therefore produced more offspring (and as we were able to feed them then it stands to reason that these tribes would have been more successful than those who were unable to provide for their family groups.) The final level of arousal is that of the spiritual experience, not just the brutish wonder of a marvellous sun rise or an appreciation for the natural world but the realisation that we are somehow connected to the world, and in turn the cosmos, in a deeper and more profound way. Consequently we have somehow inherited this behaviour either through our biological evolution, such as the fight, flight and freeze mechanism or socially from our oral and written traditions. Either way we cannot deny that Man has always pondered the meaning of existence.

I am certainly not advocating that we all have to take drugs in order for use to become more spiritually aware but it does underline the fact that even from our earliest origins we have always been preoccupied with spirituality and our connectedness to something higher than our normal everyday existences and it is my aim to attempt to unravel this most perplexing aspect of our being.

3.11 No matter what

"There will be times when you might feel weighed down or heavily burdened but please remember that it is through your tenacious efforts in struggling to scale the 'mountains of challenge' that you will experience great growth. You have unflinchingly 'wings of hope and courage!' A person bound for greatness is one who can resolutely persevere no matter what." Daisaku Ikeda.

No matter what happens to us in our lives there are two constants that remain; 1. We are responsible for getting us through times of challenge and uncertainty, and 2. We are also responsible for getting us into that situation in the first place; this is due to the strict law of causality, or the concept of Karma. Karma is the accumulation of all of the causes, both good and bad, that we have made throughout our lives which, at some point in the future (be that instantaneously or after many years) that create the effects we see in our lives in the present. Therefore, no matter what happens in our lives, good or bad, we cannot blame anyone else. Blame is such an easy, insidious and debilitating aspect of our modern lives in that it renders us completely powerless and seemingly under the control of others whims and actions. This is completely not true and we should try to remove this thinking and acting from our repertoire of responses.

When you take complete responsibility for your life you literally free yourself from the imprisonment of blame. Imagine for a moment if someone were to shackle you with chains and locks, your immediate reaction would surely be (unless you are into that kind of thing) to try to get yourself free. Someone else has imposed these restrictions on your movements and you don't like it and you are trapped by somebody else's will to restrict you, blame is like this. But it is different in that by blaming others for your misfortunes you are handing them the power of restriction and your own imprisonment, why would you want to do this? You hold the key (and the locks and chains) of your own imprisonment and therefore to your own freedom. You are ultimately the only person who is responsible whether or not you want to accept that.

Also when we allow others to control our very existence we fall foul to complete disempowerment. We ignore our internal Guru and grant those that would take advantage of our perceived helplessness to run amok. We all possess the wisdom of the ages. We all possess the ability to tap into the fundamental aspects of our lives in order to shape our futures by the causes that we make. We either accept that others have complete authority over our lives or we take that proverbial leap of faith and entrust our lives to ourselves.

3.12 A Higher Purpose

"This is the true joy of life, the being used up for a purpose recognized by yourself as a mighty one." George Bernard Shaw.

Each and every human being has the potential of tapping into a higher state of consciousness which lies above (or deeper) than our normal day to day waking state. It is a place where all that we have ever learned and all we have ever done is recorded and stored. I remember reading Terry Waite's biography, which he initially wrote in his head during his years of captivity in Beirut in the 1980's. For those of you who are unaware of Terry's story, he was sent to the Middle East by the Church of England as a peace envoy during one of its most turbulent periods in its history, the Lebanese Civil War (1975 – 1990) but was taken prisoner by those who wanted to maintain hostilities. Whilst in solitary confinement and tied to a radiator Terry obviously had vast amounts of time in which to think. He would delve into his subconscious mind and dig out as many memories as possible with as much detail as he could muster, such as the view from his school window to the smells and the sounds of his childhood and the memories that they would evoke. At some time or other we have all done this on a very simplistic level. For me it's the smell of freshly ground coffee, for others it's the smell of freshly baked bread or freshly mown grass where we are somehow transported to another time and place. Some of these memories are pleasant, some are less so, like the smell of a hospital waiting room which we most often associate with sickness or even death. What Terry was doing here was tapping into what Buddhists call the 'alaya' consciousness (the word alaya, as in Himalaya, means 'vast accumulation', 'Him' means 'snow' – thereby Himalaya literally means 'vast accumulation of snow'.) There is a term in Buddhism called 'The Nine Consciousness' which explains that above our normal senses there exists a vast accumulation of stored knowledge that, when we try, we can tap into at will.

Our five senses of sight, touch, smell, hearing and taste make up the first five levels of consciousness. Above that, the sixth level of consciousness is our logical state. When we hold an orange in our hands we know that it is an orange rather than simply an orange ball. Also if we are doing the ironing and the phone rings we don't put the iron to our ear, we answer the phone! The seventh level of consciousness is our creative consciousness where we can be doing the ironing, talking to a friend on the phone and yet still thinking about something else entirely, be it music, poetry or what you are going to eat for dinner.

The eighth level of consciousness is the 'alaya' consciousness or the storehouse consciousness where every single thought, learning and action is stored in a vast accumulation of our knowledge and wisdom. I like to think of if as rows upon rows of compact discs which have been digitally recording each and every second of our lives and that, should we know where to look, all the answers to all the questions we have ever asked are there, as do all the solutions to all of our challenges that we face. We don't have to look beyond ourselves as all the answers lie within.

I recall a proverb that goes something like this. You are sat in a single room in a vast mansion and you long to see what is in each of the other rooms. You know they exist and you can't wait to see what treasures lay beyond the confines of the space you are in. But no matter how much you try to push the door open you cannot and as your trapped feelings turn from frustration to rage you take a step back and the door that you thought open out opens within and you are free to leave the room. This is known as the ninth, and highest, level of consciousness.

In Buddhism this is called ones 'Buddhahood' but it is also known by many other names, The Sidi Consciousness or the Christ Consciousness, as within you there lays a higher realm of existence filled with ultimate wisdom, compassion and courage. Just for a moment I want you take a minute to really look within yourself and become the observer. This observer is your higher consciousness and occupies a space within you that lies somewhere between the top of your head and the soles of your feet. Right now it is observing you reading this book. It is not part of your mechanical being, it is not holding up this book for you. Nor is it part of your intellectual being, it is part of your cosmic being which, when trained, can tap into the vast realms of universal knowledge. Jungian psychologists explain this theory and use the term 'collective unconscious' to explain this common heritage, why for instance most societies share a common aversion to spiders and snakes it does not matter from what part of the world they originate. Buddhahood goes far beyond this principle as it states that every single person can reveal this Buddha nature in that it is not limited to the select or elite few.

3.13 You were meant to be happy

"Success is not the key to happiness. Happiness is the key to success. If you love what you are doing, you will be successful."
Albert Schweitzer.

Our natural state as human beings is one of comfort and stability, one of love and expression, one of abundance and unlimited creativity. Unfortunately for the vast majority of the world's population this is a mere pipe dream and not considered as realistic. Aspirations such as the concept of abundance do not seem achievable when living and dying in poverty and seem to belong to a completely different world all together let alone our own. How can one live for love when all that is seen and experienced is a world of hatred and violence? When do we have time for creativity if all we are concerned with are matters of survival and life and death? And how can we consider comfort and stability when our places of work are closing down and all we can look forward to is life on the welfare state?

However, in saying all of this, there is some good news; we are meant to be happy no matter what misfortunes may befall us. As we have touched on previously, there is no reality, there is only perception. Even if our reality is showing us extreme negativity it is merely our perception and our reactions that dictate the ultimate outcomes. For instance, if all we ever do is convince ourselves that our reality will always be in poverty, then invariably it always will be. If we convince ourselves, through our internal dialogue, that we don't deserve the good things in life then the chances are that we will never experience them and our lives will become a non ending stream of bitter disappointments. Recently a friend of mine admitted to me, and herself, that she was probably not the most good looking person and had gone through her life telling (and convincing not just herself but everyone else) that she was ugly. However she had decided to take the reverse view and to say to herself 'I don't care what anyone else thinks, I'm sound as I am. I am a nice person and I know that deep down inside I am really beautiful'. I hope you can guess what happened next, her life, and the way life treated her began to change.

We are indeed a funny lot when we know that the things that give us long-term pleasure seem to be the things that we deny ourselves the most of. We all know that it's far better to feel happy than sad but spend a larger proportion of our lives devoted to feeling sad than we do to feeling happy (the proliferation of Soap Operas is testament to this point where suffering is consumed as a means of entertainment.) We prefer peace of mind but seem to be consumed and debilitated by worry and yet, when all is said and done, for the majority of instances the buck starts and stops with ourselves and I mean this even in the most desperate of circumstances. Recently I read of an example that clearly illustrates this point. During the Second World War and all the atrocities that took place the most obvious that springs to mind has to be that of the Holocaust. One story was of a young man who saw most of his family murdered and was living under the constant threat of his own grisly demise. However this young man came to a startling realisation that the one thing that they could not take away from him was the inner workings of his own mind and rather than allow himself to be beaten he decided to rise above the atrocities and live with what he described as an 'inner dignity'. Consequently he erected a shield to combat all that was happening around him and in doing so created a space within himself where he could only be harmed if he allowed others to harm him. In essence he created his own freedom amongst so much suffering and if he was able to do this in the confinement of a Nazi concentration camp think how comparatively lucky we are. Even amongst poverty we can find richness in our lives and even during our most desperate of challenges we can find a dignity in our own existences.

3.14 Turning poison into medicine

"There are defeats more triumphant than victories." Montaigne.

There is a strange and almost perverse logic that goes something like this; sometimes the worst things that happen to us are the best things. Previously we looked at the example of Colin and Wendy Parry who lost their son Tim in the Warrington bomb and went on to establish the Warrington Peace Centre and all the good work that comes from that. Recently I read a story of a young man who completely epitomises the fact that we can seize victory from the jaws of defeat. This man loved the extremely physical sports of marathons and the ultra demanding triathlons, where the participants have to swim for miles before riding a bike for up to forty kilometres BEFORE running a full marathon of just over twenty six miles! (How tough is that?) One of the toughest triathlon events is known as the Iron Man which is held on one of the Hawaiian Islands.

The tragedy of this young man's tale is in that he was diagnosed with HIV and became extremely depressed and believing that his life was over he began to abuse his body with drink and drugs. Soon his condition worsened until he was finally diagnosed with full-blown AIDS. He told his friends that all he wanted after his death was for his ashes to be scattered over the Hawaiian Iron Man course and carried on with his abuse convincing himself that he was already dead and what was the point in trying?

Then one day he decided "No, I'm going to fight this" and stopped abusing himself and even began training by doing a little swimming and cycling. Soon he felt well enough to take a small run. As his fitness increased not only did the distance he ran increase but also his 'T' count increased (this is the number of AIDS fighting antibodies in the immune system.) He found that the more he trained not only the better he felt but the better he became. Finally he set himself the huge target of completing The Iron Man the following year. For a whole year he trained relentlessly and his doctors were astounded to see his 'T' count increasing month on month. Previously he had been given literally a matter of months to live and the people who had the same low 'T' count as him before he began to train were beginning to die. He was not only the only survivor but had set new standards in longevity.

Finally the day came when he completed The Iron Man and within a week had exactly the same 'T' count as any other healthy person. He was obviously overjoyed but the doctors were far more astounded and delivered a statement which said that this man had virtually "cured himself of AIDS" through courage, determination and hard work. The young man in question also said that being diagnosed with HIV and then AIDS was "probably the best thing that could have happened to me!" There are countless other examples of these 'miracles'. One only has to read the biography of the cyclist Lance Armstrong to realise this. Lance was diagnosed with cancer yet went on to become a seven times winner of the prestigious and ultra-demanding Tour de France. Our attitude is everything. It can turn even our disasters into triumphs and what seemed like poison into medicine.

3.15 Self Empowerment

"A thoroughly good relationship with ourselves results in being still, which doesn't mean we don't run and jump and dance about. It means there's no compulsiveness. We don't overwork, overeat, oversmoke, overseduce. In short, we begin to stop causing harm." Pema Chodron

The ultimate expression of self empowerment has got to be taking ultimate responsibility for ones own life. Even in the face of overwhelming medical evidence where these people were told by eminent experts that they were soon going to die these courageous men took responsibility for their own lives and decided to empower themselves rather than allowing the doctors opinions to prevail. If they had they would soon have died, instead they turned their lives around and became shining examples of self empowerment.

Self empowerment is literally giving yourself the power to create and manifest your own future the way you see it regardless of those who say it can't be done or that it's impossible or by the sceptical distracters that say "Are you crazy?" or "Who do you think you are?" If we were all to allow these people's opinions to prevail then some of man's greatest achievements would not have come to pass. If Michelangelo had listened to those that said "You want to take how many years lying on your back painting a ceiling?" we would not have the Cistene Chapel. If the Wright brothers had listened to those that said "If God had intended man to fly he would have given us wings" we would not have the opportunity to travel the world. Self empowerment not only has the power to create benefit in our own lives but also the power to create benefit for all. It is one of the most precious gifts that we give ourselves and at the same time give to the rest of the world.

Imagine for a moment if we were able to meet ourselves 'Mk 2', our 'doppelganger', us but not us, the same in every aspect, with the same hopes, fears, aspirations and challenges. Now, this person has come to ask our advice, what type of language would we choose to use? Would we be scathing? Would we say that they should forget trying to accomplish anything in their lives as it will only lead to disappointment? I think not. We would probably be warm and supportive. We would be understanding and encouraging, would we not? We would probably listen to their concerns and offer the best advice that we could by letting them realise that they are special and that no matter what they are currently going through they are bound to find an answer due to their unique talents. So why is it that we don't do this to ourselves? Why is it that our own internal dialogue is often self-destructive? Why do we put ourselves down during times of uncertainty when what we should be doing is comforting and encouraging ourselves? Why do we disempower ourselves when we would offer support if we were meeting ourselves Mk 2? Think about it.

Throughout the process of writing this book I have studied a great many books on the subject of self-empowerment and found that the constant theme that runs throughout these volumes remains, that by taking the reins of our own existence we begin to steer it in the direction that we choose. It's not about handing authority over to others it's all about the individual taking control of their own lives and part of this comes down to empowering oneself through finding faith.

FAITH

As soon as most people hear the word faith they tend to go running scared and conjure up images of pious religious dedication where they have to appease themselves at the feet of some almighty being and participate in all manner of bizarre acts of self sacrifice. Faith is far more than a mere religious practice as it lies at the very root of our spirituality and faith in ourselves and our own abilities. So why is it considered alright to have faith in oneself but passé to have faith in our beliefs? I firmly believe, along with countless others, that the lack of faith in our spirituality is one of the prime reasons behind mans seemingly continual decline into intolerance and barbarity. Some would argue that religious faith is one of the main reasons for conflict and intolerance but, as we will discuss, this depends on whether or not that religious belief is inclusive or exclusive, whether or not it preaches tolerance and togetherness or separateness and division.

Over the decades and indeed the centuries and millennia we have, as a species, moved away from our common spiritual heritage and in doing so have denied one of our most fundamental aspects of our existence, that being that we are highly evolved creatures who are capable of creating what could be described as the unimaginable. Yet we have seemed to have convinced ourselves that we are somehow no more than cattle. Could this be the reason why in many parts of the world human life is considered so cheap?

Let us once more take a step back and look into our deepest past where as a species we possessed a far greater acceptance of spirituality. Early man's first buildings were more often than not erected as a symbol of gratitude to some external force, be that the Sun or the Moon or the 'gods' of the seasons. These monuments stood as symbols of praise and signs of gratitude towards those things that put food in their bellies and clothes on their backs.

If we move forward a little more in history ALL the ancient civilisations had a deep and intuitive understanding of matters spiritual and praised all manner of beings, from the natural to the supernatural.

So why is it that we have moved away from praise towards scepticism and even downright hostility? Why is it that we have turned our backs on faith in preference to science? It has been said many times that science has become the new religion but what does that mean? It is true that we need our questions answered yet we now put our faith in science to provide those answers when faith was getting on fine without science for thousands of years. Before I continue, let me make it perfectly clear that I am not dismissing science all together, nor am I advocating creationist theory over evolutionary theory. What I am attempting to explain is that there exists a meeting of the two seemingly polar extremes and that science is now catching up with some beliefs that have existed for longer than the word science itself. Science is merely the process of providing empirical and peer reviewed evidence to validate a particular theory whereas faith is wrongly considered as substance without proof. Or as one great scientist put it:

> "There is no necessary conflict between science and religion if the nature of religion is properly understood." Albert Einstein.

When reading through these next sections I want you, for the time being at least, to put any scepticism that you may possess on hold and to momentarily suspend your disbelief into believing that each and every one of us holds within us the spark of the divine. Let's face it we all suspend our disbelief every time we sit down to watch a film. We suspend the disbelief that what we are seeing is more than just coloured lights on a flat screen. If we were not able to do this none of us would ever enjoy a story told in this way. Faith is far more real than a movie and a fundamental aspect towards creating and maintaining balance in our lives.

3.21 There is no Almighty

"Alas, the fearful Unbelief is unbelief in yourself." Thomas Carlyle.

To some this may come as no surprise, to others it will be considered as blasphemous however, in terms of self empowerment, the whole concept of some Almighty Being residing over the workings of our lives and the workings of the whole of universal life has to be the epitome of disempowerment. The only God that exists is the god of one's own making. There is however a world of difference between having a faith and having a god where having a faith is akin to self empowerment whereas having a god is akin to disempowerment. Put another way if you believe that our lives and subsequently all the events of our lives are controlled by some all powerful being then what we are practicing is a belief that we have no control what-so-ever over our actions and therefore our life. However, if we have faith in our own abilities as an able human being and take direct responsibility for our actions then we are practicing a philosophy of self value and control. Also, by creating a concept of higher and lesser beings we have just planted the seeds of conflict in that we have introduced the concept of separateness, of an 'us' and 'them', of a right and a wrong.

Another way of explaining this point is in terms of fate, destiny and karma. Fatalists would have us believe that one cannot control ones fate. If we are fated to die in a crash then that is our fate and we can do nothing about it. Also, if it is our destiny to become rich then this will automatically happen, regardless of us applying any real effort. It is like the history of our lives is already written on the day we are born and will remain unchangeable until the day that we die. I imagine an accountant like number-crunching god busy tapping away on some giant celestial computer arranging our every move, what utter nonsense! What of free will? What of choice? And what of causality? Surely we have more control over our lives?

The answer to this conundrum lies in the explanation of the concept of karma. As already mentioned karma strictly adheres to the universal law of cause and effect and thereby states that we can dramatically influence our outcomes by our own actions. Instead of passing the buck and handing responsibility elsewhere karma is rooted in our taking direct responsibility and realising that our actions in the present dictate our outcomes in the future. We have effectively taken control over our lives by taking control of our actions. However karma goes further to explain that there is no such thing as 'immutable karma' in that no matter what we have done in the past we can still have a say in our future. There is no crime of misdemeanour too great that we cannot overcome this negativity by making good causes in the present and taking positive action in and for the future. To illustrate this point, the life of the ex IRA terrorist Patrick McGee comes to mind. Patrick McGee was the man who planted the Brighton bomb at the Conservative party conference (October 12th 1984) and was directly responsible for the murder and permanent injury of dozens of people. Here is a man who has killed and maimed in the most hideous of ways yet now he spends his time as a dedicated peace activist. Not only is he healing the wounds of a shattered community who have been traumatised for generations but he is also healing his own negative karma. Some would say that if he has killed he deserves to die but, in his living, if he can save the lives of others then surely he has the right to try? I have no sympathy for terrorists but I have compassion for human beings that have been driven to committing atrocities as their only means of their expression of grievances.

3.22 Finding a faith

"How many a man has dated a new era in his life from the reading of a book?" Thoreau.

So, why is faith so important and how do we go about finding a faith that works both for us and for the world at large? First of all let us consider why faith is so important and how it can become a driving force in our lives rather than a debilitating distraction. If we look back in history we see our world being shaped by men (and of course women) of faith. I think in positive terms of The Reverend Martin Luther King and Ghandi who were both men of faith and men who had huge and significant social and moral impact upon their times. Without their faith they would not have had the courage of their convictions that their actions were justified and without their actions the world we live in would probably be a darker and less tolerant one. The flip side of this is of course those who have, through their (misguided) faith, destroyed more than created in their inflated state of complete self righteousness. The Spanish Conquistadors, Pol Pot and Saddam Hussein come to mind as each believing that they were so right that those who did not believe what they believed should simply be eliminated.

This is the old argument, it has been said that more wars have been created in the name of religion than by anything else. In some ways this perception may be true but I disagree with the sentiment in other aspects. For instance, at the time of writing this, the so called War on Terror in Iraq is raging and some would argue that this is indeed a religious conflict, or 'Jihad', it is however apparent to a great many people that the main reasons behind the conflict are purely economic (as were the root causes of the twentieth century's greatest massacre, known more commonly as The First World War!) Hundreds of people everyday are (and millions in the past have) died in the name of commerce and the price of a barrel of oil which tragically continues to this very day. Those that worship at this altar do so without regard for either the sanctity of human life but also the fragile essence of our global environment (the recent Deep Water Horizon oil spill in the Gulf of Mexico springs to mind.) They rape and pillage both, not in the name of faith, but in the name of profit. These are far from enlightened actions for the mutual benefit of all but narrow, self-serving and destructive for the benefit of only the sick and twisted poisoned by greed, arrogance and ignorance.

Faith in the name of mutual benefit is completely different. Faith in the name of 'if I win, we all win' resounds in the words of both Martin Luther King and Ghandi. Their struggles were the struggles of all humanity and their victories belong to everyone. Again the difference comes when we consider faiths in terms of being either inclusive or exclusive. An inclusive faith is as it sounds in that it includes rather than excludes. An exclusive faith is limited to the elite with their costumes and ceremonies and time-served status. An inclusive faith is for the benefit of everyone whereas an exclusive faith is only for the benefit of the few. An inclusive faith is one that requires no special skills or qualifications whereas an exclusive faith is one that requires years of pious dedication and relies on hierarchy and rank.

So, on one hand, faith is very important but on the other hand seemingly very difficult to find. My advice would be similar to that of finding an exercise routine or diet that suits you as one that sits comfortably with your current mores and values. I know that when I first started practicing Buddhism I found it very easy to accept this profound philosophy as it was close to being what I had always believed. I was working on a writing project with a man who was practicing and with us spending a lot of time in close proximity and being curious, we talked a lot about his faith. In doing so I found that my current values already matched the values of Buddhism and was pleased to know that there was actually a name for what I believed was always true. For me it was the Buddhism of Nichiren Daishonin, for you it may be something else, all I suggest is that you open your life to the infinite possibilities that you can empower yourself to the point of the miraculous should you find a faith. So long as it enriches rather than diminishes what you will find on that road of your unique journey will be of value to yourself and for everyone else that you encounter.

3.23 Faith = Courage = Purpose

"A life lived without purpose or value, the kind in which one doesn't know the reason why one was born, is joyless and lacklustre. To just live, eat and die without any real sense of purpose surely represents a life pervaded by the world of animality. On the other hand, to do, create or contribute something that benefits others, society and ourselves and to dedicate ourselves as long as we live up to that challenge-that is a life of true satisfaction, a life of value. It is a humanistic and lofty way to live." Daisaku Ikeda.

The reason why faith is so important is that it enables you to possess the wisdom in order to make the right decisions so that you have the courage to take the right actions; it's as simple as that. Or in the words of the famous saying;

"Grant me the serenity to accept the things I cannot change, the courage to change the things I can, and the wisdom to know the difference." Reinhold Niebuhr.

To be empowered by a faith that gives you power over your own future is to hand yourself the key to your own freedom. Once you have found your faith you then become more acutely tuned in to the heartbeat of the universe and in doing so enable yourself to become a conduit to its powers. The current of life will then run through your veins giving you the chance to obtain your wisdom from some higher source. This energy is simultaneously of you as well as beyond you. It is both of your own making yet the grand design lies elsewhere.

When you open yourself up to the possibility that you can tune yourself into this higher energy you allow yourself the luxury of not having to merely think your way out of a situation. When you possess a profound philosophy on life you awaken previously dormant aspects of your life where you can move beyond the mere physical into the higher realms of existence. Sometimes there is nothing worse than pacing the floor trying to work out a solution to a challenge within the confines of your mind. All you tend to do is to continually turn over the problem again and again without any real solutions offering themselves. This can lead to the problem seeming all the greater as no solutions seem to fit the circumstances. Panic sets in, your thought processes are even more hindered and the whole thing becomes an ever more depreciating vicious cycle. Surely it would seem a better solution to not to have to think about it and use a more reliable source of wisdom to provide the answers?

This wisdom stems from possessing strong faith. The wisdom of the ages and of countless generations applying a tried and tested formula yielding results again and again. When I have a challenge to overcome and seemingly insurmountable problems what I do is to try and stop thinking, take myself to a place of tranquillity (either through chanting, meditating or going outdoors to a peaceful spot) and surrender to the universe. By this I mean I allow myself to plunge into the ocean of innate and eternal wisdom that is both of myself and beyond myself and all of a sudden, what once seemed like a problem without solution, new ideas come to mind. By forgetting about it, I remember. By surrendering, I conquer and by switching off my brain, the lights go on. The great thing about doing this once is that you can do it again and again knowing that it is a power that can never diminish, a technique that has a myriad of applications and a means to knowing that there is no such thing as a problem without a solution. It's also about trusting your Guru wisdom.

3.24 Not blind faith

"If a man will begin with certainties he shall end in doubts, but if he will be content to begin with doubts he shall end in certainties."
Francis Bacon.

Any belief, philosophy or religion that states 'this is the way that it is and that's all there is to it!' to me is on a road to nowhere. Why is it that we have beliefs in the first place if not to answer our basic questions such as 'Why?' If the answer is simply 'because that's the way it is' then to me, that is simply not good enough. Many religions state that there's no point in questioning 'the Lord' or they state that the word of God is final and that 'He moves in mysterious ways', to me that is the ultimate cop out and cause for suspicion. For a belief to work it must be open to scrutiny and be able to supply some kind of proof, otherwise it is merely one persons view prevailing over someone else's. (There are plenty of words to describe this kind of philosophy including indoctrination, propaganda, subjugation and dictatorship).

For a belief to work it must satisfy what is known as the three types of proof; theoretical proof, documentary proof and actual proof. The first, theoretical proof is as it sounds, a philosophy that makes some sort of sense on a theoretical level. (i.e. 'We can become better than we are' rather than the impracticality of saying 'we can fly like a bird') The second proof is documentary proof, i.e. is there any written evidence to substantiate the claim that we can 'become better than we are'? Also is this material available for everyone to not only scrutinise and study, but also to question as well as understand? Or is it hidden away in some kind of sacred vault where only the high priests or the holy men are allowed access? (If so then beware!) Thirdly and probably most importantly, can we measure actual proof from application through to reward? And if not, then are we merely making up the result in order to fit our expectations?

At this point you will be in one of four camps. 1. You will already possess a faith in which you have no doubts. 2. You have a faith in which you have doubts. 3. You are questioning the need for a faith, or 4. You accept the need to find a faith but still have doubts. If you are in camp 1 then all I have to say is well done. If you are in camp 2 then I will also say well done for you now have the opportunity to really test your faith. If you are in camp 3 I will say a couple of things. One is that you ought to open your mind a little and be prepared to test and validate something before you dismiss it all together. Before I found my faith I was exactly the same. I felt as though faith and religion had no part in my life and the only people that needed the crutch of faith were the weak and pathetic. (What I have found since is completely the opposite as the people of faith that I know are immensely strong and resilient.) The second, and last, thing to say is that it probably won't matter what I say because if your mind is made up (or closed) then what ever I say will be glossed over until you read something else that strikes your chord! Finally if you are in camp 4 – keep reading!

Faith is not a burden to carry but a way to lighten your load. It is not an arduous task to be done but a pleasure to be performed. It's not about being shackled it's about being free. Some would even say that they are too hedonistic to consider giving up their pleasure seeking ways for the sake of some higher cause like tuning into some higher energy or creating the building blocks for world peace, mistakenly thinking that they will have to give something up in order to move forward. Here's the rub, freeing yourself is probably one of the most hedonistic things that you could probably ever do. If you don't want to do it for someone, or something else, then at least do it for you!

3.25 Guru-You

"Men talk about Bible miracles because there is no miracle in their lives. Cease to gnaw that crust. There is ripe fruit over your head."
Thoreau.

What a sad thing to realise that there is no miracle in life! What a shameful waste of existence not to know that ones living and breathing is indeed a miracle in itself. I think what Thoreau was trying to say was that some people turn to religions for all the wrong reasons, their lives seem so dull and meaningless that in order to feel part of a grander scheme they turn to 'The Bible' or any other works of religious scripture. They do so to feel empowered by a greater external source yet in doing so are disempowering themselves from the true source. Cease to gnaw on that crust! For this is not the way it is. In each of us there lies a spark of the divine. We all possess a unique entity which is as individual as our own DNA yet at the same time part of a collective whole that binds everything together.

Within you there resides an entity which I have entitled 'Your Own Personal Guru' who is there to provide all the answers to all of the questions you have ever asked. A source of limitless resources that is on the job twenty-four hours a day seven days a week 'at your service'. In terms of Buddhism, it is one's Buddhahood or enlightened state. This Guru has been, and will continue to be, your constant companion on this journey we call life. Your Guru possesses all the wisdom you need ever have as to what makes you not only who you are and how you are made up, but also what you are capable of, as well as how to best accomplish it.

In terms of faith, Guru–U is all about having faith in yourself and your own innate abilities to construct your own futures for yourself (haven't you got the point by now??) It's not a very subtle point that I am trying to make but let me say it in another way in case you haven't quite understood yet. There is nobody standing in the way of your ambitions other than you. There is no one else limiting your potential other than the person you see in the mirror every day. Conversely there is one person that can assist you in fulfilling your desires, that self same person that you feed and clean and clothe. If you feel the need to project your thoughts on someone other than yourself then just consider this. You have a Guru inside pulling the levers and flicking the switches of your controls. He or she is an absolute expert whose timing is impeccable. He or she knows both exactly what to press as well as precisely when to press them. So, have ultimate faith in your own abilities as well as opening yourself up to the possibility that you are capable of far much more than you ever thought possible.

3.26 Visualisation

"Projecting your mind into a successful situation is the most powerful means to achieve goals. If you spend time with pictures of failure in your mind you orchestrate failure." Estee Lauder.

The pictures that we see in our minds are the same ones that we project on the screen we call our lives. What you paint internally colours your reality. If your colours are vibrant on the inside you can bet that your life will be filled with light. If it is dull and drab and filled with gloom and doom then guess what? (I'm sure you 'get the picture'). Estee Lauder put it right, by painting successful mental pictures you stand a far greater chance of fulfilling that success compared to someone who has already convinced themselves that their venture is bound to end in tears. Although possessing a positive outlook is by no means a guarantee to success it certainly gives us a far better chance of succeeding. If we wake up with 'a new day brings new promise' type of attitude rather than a 'here we go again' one, surely we are bound to start on the right footing.

We have previously discussed how meditation is an excellent source of stress reduction there is however a whole lot more to it than that. Meditation is probably one of the most efficient means of exercising your mind to prepare it for the prolonged rigours of existence. It builds fortitude as well as resilience. It clears the mind of all other distractions and focuses your complete attention to the matters in hand again, without having to really think about them. Expanding yourself spiritually through practising spiritual exercises is no different to expanding yourself physically through physical exercises.

I remember an exercise that I was once taught by my Qi Gong Master and it is certainly something that you could easily try yourself. All you have to do is to sit on a chair with your back straight, your eyes closed and your hands on your knees (palms up to maintain the flow of chi). Next completely free your mind of any distractions and then place yourself in this space. Then all you have to do is imagine yourself as being completely happy and then feel the way you would feel when all of your ambitions and dreams have become reality. This is a very easy yet profoundly peculiar exercise as your emotional responses may well range from tears to laughter. I have utilised this technique on numerous occasions and have sometimes found myself filled with such a sense of relief that I have burst into tears. At other times I have been grinning from ear to ear not wanting to come down from my high when the exercise was finally over.

This is a great way of painting positive pictures in our minds as it enables us to visualise our own independent interpretation on what it means to be successful and content. This in turn creates an internal cause deep within our lives which creates the fuel for the fire that leads to their eventual physical manifestations. It is as inevitable as cause and effect itself. We begin with a latent cause (i.e. all of our dreams and ambitions) this leads to an internal cause being made (visualisations, determinations) this then creates a latent effect in the physical world which, given appropriate action and time, creates the manifest effect, our ambitions are satisfied and our dreams become our reality.

HOPE

"If it were not for hope, the heart would break." Thomas Fuller.

What would our worlds be like if they were devoid of hope? I use the plural here to illustrate that we occupy two worlds, the world of the microcosm (i.e. our own singular and internal world) and the world of the macrocosm (i.e. the world we share with the billions of other human beings.) Hope is the quintessentially human characteristic that drives us onward and upward. It is the driving force behind our motivations towards creating a life less ordinary for ourselves, our families, as well as our communities, societies, and ultimately our race. *'Without hope, the heart would break'* for without hope what future would we have to look forward to?

Hope provides you with an aim towards some kind of certainty and security in an uncertain and seemingly chaotic world. If you were not to hope for a better future then you would lose your aim towards creating one. Like in the words of the old song *'If you don't have a dream, how are you going to have a dream come true?'* If you don't have a vision of a hopeful future then what have you got to look forward to? If you are struggling and you believe that next year is going to be as hard as the year before then guess what? You are probably going to be right. If you are suffering from a terrible illness and you convince yourself that there is no hope for you and that you are bound to die, then guess what? You probably will. In fact time and time again medical science has been dumbfounded by those people who have been told that they are going to die only to prove the doctors wrong by living which stems from their unshakeable hope that they will survive and in doing so, do so. Conversely nothing is more certain of failure than convincing yourself that it's impossible.

Emerson wrote that *"Hope puts us in a working mood"* and unless we have something to work towards then we will never be in a position to work towards improving our situation or circumstances. Hope also allows us to possess sufficient wisdom in order for us not to be impatient. It has been said many times by many people that 'anything worth achieving for is worth working for'. Nothing in life, at least of any worth, is ever accomplished without a degree of persistence and perseverance and if it were not for hope we would tend to give up when the going gets tough. Unless we have a clear vision of a hopeful future, then what is it that will keep us on track towards that future when we are clouded by doubt or seemingly insurmountable obstacles are in our way? Hope is both the compass and the beacon in the darkness that lead us forward to a brighter future. Therefore when we keep the flame of hope burning bright we stand a far better chance of reaching our destination.

3.31 Keep your eye on the prize

"Men trip not on mountains but on stones." Hindustani proverb.

We all have our own unique vision in our minds of what it is that we require from life in order to be really, really happy (at least I hope you do by now!) To be so content and fulfilled where every day is part of the adventure and we revel in our very own existence. A place and a time where all of our problems have found solutions, all challenges overcome, wishes granted and the prospect of a future filled with limitless possibilities lies before us. Discoveries to be made, treasures to be found and peace in your heart. (It sounds great doesn't it?) We have this vision of the future at one level and our own current level of existence at another and inevitably a gap between the two, so how do we close that gap and bring forward our happiness? How do we speed up the process of fulfilling our desires and creating long-term diamond like happiness? I suggest that this is by first of all knowing who we are, knowing what we want from life (in detail) and realising that we have to take action in order to bring forward that date when we are finally content.

To do this you have to, not only keep your eye on the prize but know exactly what the prize is. (I hope by reading this book so far you now have already picked up one or two ways for you to do this.) By applying some of these ideas you will certainly know yourself a lot better and by expanding yourself (physically, emotionally and spiritually) your rate of progress cannot help but increase. And by disciplining yourself towards continually applying your own success formula you will go a long way to ensuring your success. By knowing yourself, expanding yourself and disciplining yourself you are already taking the direct action necessary for speeding up the process. What I mean by process is the perceived inevitability of getting where you need to be most and allowing events to somehow carry you there. There are three possible outcomes here; 1. You will reach your destination as a matter of fate without really having to try. 2. You are destined to fail so what's the point in trying? Or 3. You can change your Karma by taking the actions to fulfil your dreams.

This way you will always have, not only a clear definition of what it is that you want and where you want to be, but also a precise plan of action as to how you are going to get there. And then, no matter what happens, no matter what misfortunes may befall you or seemingly insurmountable objects are placed in your way you will be able to find a way through these times and around the obstacles via an alternative route to the place you know you have to, and will, be. Happiness is a destination and getting there is the journey we call life so therefore it is extremely important that you also enjoy the journey, as well as taking time to admire the view along the way.

An interesting way to do this is to imagine yourself at your eightieth birthday party talking with friends and family and looking back on your life well lived. How you constructed your success and how you dealt with your disappointments. Personally I have a vision of the map of my own future which lasts up until my eighty-fifth birthday (over forty years from now!) and the milestones in between are spaced seven years apart. In the Buddhist calendar there are many significant events and times, one of which is known as 'The Seven Bells'. These bells, each one lasting for a period of seven years, herald significant times in the history and development of mankind and mark our own personal history in conjunction with being alive at this time. This significant period in our history is right now at the beginning of the twenty-first century (up to the year 2050) and the one thing that all the people alive in the world at this time have in common is that we are all alive at the same time! Which is both obvious and significant as it begs the questions as to why we have chosen to be alive at this time and what are we going to do about it?

3.32 The difference between believing and knowing

"Never try to be an intellectual, but always try to possess intellect."
Dr. M. Hatsumi

The difference between believing and knowing is subtle yet profound for in its understanding lies the secret to manifesting your future in the present. Understanding the difference between believing and knowing lies at the very core of the question that separates the 'us as we are' life-state and our 'Guru' life-state, in that it asks do you truly believe and know that such a life-state exists at all? If you believe that this elevated life state may well be possible but are unsure that it actually does then you are no better off than when you started reading this than you were before, or are you? Or have you looked within yourself to realise that you are indeed a unique creative being who has an equally unique contribution towards providing happiness for yourself and others?

So, how does knowing that this is the case mean we can manifest your future in the present? When you know that the actions you are taking are having a positive impact on your life in the present and you know that the outcomes will therefore work in your favour in the future you then create a deep connection with the inevitability of your success in life. And when you feel this and know it to be true, you can manifest the exact emotions of how you would feel at that time in the future right now in the present. (See 3.26 Visualisation.) This is also part of the enjoying the journey as much as reaching the destination, because, let's face it the journey is a life-long one and even when you have fulfilled your desires and all of your dreams have become reality, then there will always be new experiences and challenges that you will wish to pursue. There is nothing sadder than a person working all of their lives towards building their dream and, after wearing themselves out along the way, to get there and think "I'm bored now!" You must learn to savour and appreciate the present and in doing so your contentment is assured in as much as you will already be experiencing what it is that you want to achieve and that connection with your future happiness will show itself in the present.

When you believe that something may happen then you might be right, but when you know that something is going to happen (and you make it happen) then you *know* you are right. In Buddhist philosophy this is known as the difference between learning and realisation. You can study all you want and read countless volumes but unless you have realised what you have learned then you have not reached a deeper understanding than before you studied. I'm sure you are familiar with plenty of well educated people that still have extreme difficulty with the rudiments of holding even a simple conversation (in fact in some cases it seems exponentially proportional that the longer the education the shorter the conversation!) Learning and all the joys and discoveries that it can bring, is one thing, putting it into practice and seeing tangible results is something else entirely.

This is not to say that you should not study, quite the contrary, unless you learn you cannot realise, but Dr. Hatsumi put it so eloquently when he said *"Never try to be an intellectual but always try to possess intellect."* He meant that you should always strive to be more than you are but not to limit what you may become. If you get too specialised in one area then the only people who will understand you are fellow specialists in that area. Have you ever noticed how people from certain professions stick together? Archaeologists befriend archaeologists. Theoretical physicists hang around with other theoretical physicists. You must try to become more rounded if you are to become grounded enough for your wisdom to be of benefit to all and not just the few.

3.33 Taking action

"Until one is committed there is hesitancy, the chance to draw back, always ineffectiveness. Concerning all acts of initiative (and creation) there is one elementary truth, the ignorance of which kills countless ideas and splendid plans: the moment one definitely commits oneself, then providence moves too. All sorts of things occur to help one that would otherwise never have occurred. A whole stream of events issues from that decision, raising in one's favour all manner of unforeseen incidents and meetings and material assistance, which no man could have dreamed would have come his way." W.N. Murray.

So, how committed are you to ensuring your own success? There is only one person you have to be honest with here and that is yourself. In this instant nobody else matters and the decisions you have made, or are about to make, or won't make can only be made by, and for, you. Are you committed to making a plan of action for your balance and happiness and then are you committed to taking the necessary action? (And if not, why not?) What have you got to lose and what have you got to gain? Most people hold themselves back from moving forward out of fear of the unknown, fear that they may somehow lose something of themselves along the way. But surely it's worse to lose the uncertainty of not knowing the outcome than to gain the certainty of the outcome being nothing? Some people, believe it or not, actually make the deliberate act of choosing to be lazy and to forever remain ignorant of their potential.

As Eli Cohen puts it so succinctly *"Without continuous personal development you are now all that you will ever become, and hell starts when the person you are meets the person you could have been."*

To me there is no greater crime than the one perpetrated against yourself than this, ignorance by accident is one thing, ignorance by design is something else entirely and the moment you choose to not deliberately commit yourself to your personal development then you certainly are guilty as charged! Thank you for reading the book and goodnight sleep well!

Or, have you finally decided to wake up and take the bull by the horns? Have you decided that it's time, now more than ever, to roll up your sleeves and do the hard work necessary? To try and, in the trying, to succeed? Have you decided that enough is enough and that the time has now come for you to get exactly what you want from life? And if so, CONGRATULATIONS!!! You have just taken the first steps towards a brighter future.

When you ask from the universe, the universe responds. When you work in harmony with the universe, the universe provides and when you open yourself up to the infinite possibilities of the universe then the universe will reveal its limitless potential to and for you. All you have to do is to commit yourself to yourself and to take the actions that are necessary and to realise that the actions that you have decided to take do not run contrary to your values or your inherent abilities. As I have said before, when given a choice, rarely do people choose to do something that they find abhorrent or counter to their existing talents. *"A one legged man will never win an ass-kicking competition!"* Remember that you are unique and special and that you carry your own sense of purpose towards creating a grand vision of your future filled with happiness, balance and contentment.

3.34 Trust in Guru-U

"The really great make you feel that you too can become great."
Mark Twain.

Everybody, no matter how rich or poor, young or old, successful or otherwise responds to praise. (See Human Givens – Recognition) Isn't it great when someone says to us "well done" or "that was great" or "we couldn't have done it without you"? When your contribution is valued you feel more inclined to contribute. When you are appreciated your sense of appreciation in others also increases and when you see the greatness in others you realise how great you are. And here's the truth of the matter: YOU ARE GREAT!!

You must realise that you carry within you a spark of the divine and the possibility to really make a difference, not only in terms of your own happiness but also with regards to the happiness of others. This special inner being I have described as your own personal Guru, but guess what? It was you all along! If you trust in your own abilities then you trust in Guru-U and vice-versa, if you implicitly trust Guru-U you unquestioningly trust yourself which I believe is the ultimate gift that you can give yourself. It is the golden key to your own freedom and the permission for you to be anything that you have always wanted to be.

Most people place this authority outside themselves and give this power to someone else believing that they are somehow not worthy and that only the elite are qualified to be called a Guru, what utter tosh! This is a myth that has been perpetrated by those who wish to control others (usually for the sake of profit or because of their own inflated egos) but there is only one person that allows this myth to go unchallenged by not questioning its validity. You perpetuate the myth by unconditionally accepting it to be true. But let me tell you here and now, there is no Guru outside of yourself unless you wish there to be so! And all you have to do is to suspend your disbelief that this is the case, accept the fact that you are best qualified to find your own direction and balance in life and to realise that you possess the infinite wisdom to be able to move your life forward to achieve whatever it is in life that will bring you balance, contentment and happiness. All you have to do is to know yourself, be yourself and trust yourself.

Trust that all of the answers lie within. Trust that all of the solutions to your challenges will show themselves when the time is right and trust that there is no such thing as a problem that cannot be overcome by your own actions. You are not only the key holder but also the key maker. You are no longer a slave to someone else's theories but the master of your own choices. You need no longer just look outside yourself for the answers but to look inside yourself, and trust that whenever you question you have the innate knowledge to provide the solutions.

As I have stated before, this is not meant to devalue the input of others and the learning that we can get from those that have trodden the path before us, far from it. But when you really take the time to get to know yourself and to dedicate yourself to this most noble of causes and then to realise that only you can do it and that ultimately it is a journey that only you can take alone. Others can help you along the way by providing a map or a compass but it's only you that can do the exercises if you want to get fit. It's only you that can take the medicine if you want to get better and it's only you that can discover yourself and that everyone else are the tools that we utilise in our own creation (and to be thankful for their wanting to help!)

EPILOGUE

Throughout my career in training and development I've encountered a single saying which remains as a fundamental block towards any progress in the workplace which is the expression "That's the way it's always been done." In my capacity of a Lean Manufacturing Consultant when analysing why processes are carried out in a particular fashion it's a saying I hear all too often – 'That's the way it's always been done' often with no thought as to whether or not this is in fact the most efficient way of accomplishing a task. I'm sure it's an expression that you would have come across at some time or another but it surprises me that this logic is never really challenged and quite readily accepted as the norm.

However a behavioural experiment on chimpanzees beautifully illustrates this point – an experiment known as 'the Five Monkeys';

Take five chimpanzees and put them into a cage. In the cage there is a set of step ladders and suspended just above the step ladders, within easy reach, is a bunch on bananas. What do you think happens? This is not a trick question – the first idea that came into your head may well be the correct one. It obvious; they'll take a look at the bunch of bananas, see the ladder and think 'Oh, a bunch of bananas. I'm going to climb that ladder and have some!' But as soon as one of them touches the ladder they all get sprayed with cold water, which of course they don't like, in fact they hate it as they associate water with discomfort which is akin to pain, so they stop doing it.

A couple of minutes later one of them looks up, sees the bunch of bananas and the ladder enticing them to climb and thinks 'Oh, a bunch of bananas' and as soon as they touch the ladder they all get sprayed again. After a while they begin to figure it out – don't go near the ladders as that equals pain/discomfort.

Once this behaviour has been established within the group and not one of the chimps goes near the ladder you take out one of them and place in a brand new chimp – what do you thinks happens? Again, not a trick question. The new chimp sees the bunch of bananas and a set of step ladders leading up to them and thinks 'Oh, a bunch of bananas. I'll have some of them!' Now at this point there is no longer any water involved. There is no punishment from the outside; the consequences are now within the group. As soon as the new chimp touches the ladders the rest of the group beat him up! They are so used to the pain/discomfort of the water that they will stop anyone breaking that rule with as much force as is necessary, often resorting to violence!

So the new chimp takes a beating, shuffles off into a corner of the cage and licks his wounds. After a while (as chimp's memories are not very long) it looks up and sees a bunch of bananas and thinks 'Oh, a bunch of bananas' and as soon as he goes to touch the ladder he gets beaten up again. This process repeats itself for a few more times until eventually the chimp gets the message – don't go near the ladder as it equals pain.

Once this behaviour has been ingrained take out one of the original five chimps and replace him with a new one; what do you think happens? Again, the obvious. The new chimp sees the bananas and heads straight for the ladders and the rest of the group, you've guessed it, beat him up, including the chimp that has never been wet!

Again this process repeats itself until the new chimp eventually gets the message – don't go near the ladders as it equals pain.

Now follow this sequence to its logical conclusion where in turn each of the original five chimpanzees have been removed from the cage and all that are left are five chimps who have never been wet but will never go near the set of ladders to retrieve the bananas. Why – BECAUSE THAT'S THE WAY IT'S ALWAYS BEEN DONE!!

Come on. We're not chimpanzees, we're human beings! But we still live by that very same adage; that's the way it's always been done, without ever asking ourselves why and questioning whether or not it is this the most efficient way of doing things?

So, in conclusion, remove this excuse from your repertoire; just because that's the way it's always been done doesn't always make it right. Sometimes it's just the law of the group, but that doesn't always make it right and returning to the old adage 'If you always do what you've always done you will always get what you've always got'. So if you want to change your outcomes you have first got to change your approach!

I hope that these ideas have given you plenty of your own and that from now on you will be able to find greater balance and harmony in your lives. I pray that the guidance offered within these pages will lead you to a life well lived and that all of you dreams become reality.

Live well.
Live long.
Love well.
Love long.

"To laugh often and much; to win the respect of intelligent people and the affection of children; to earn the appreciation of honest criticism and endure the betrayal of false friends; to appreciate beauty and find the best in others; to leave the world a bit better; ...to know that one life has breathed easier because you have lived – this is to have succeeded." Ralph Waldo Emerson.

PAUL WILSON BONNER is a Business Training & Development Consultant based in Kendal in England's beautiful Lake District. A former Martial Arts teacher, he has been a practising Buddhist for many years and applies the practical and personal developmental aspects of Buddhist teachings to business methodologies and team structures within his consultancy work.

www.ingramcontent.com/pod-product-compliance
Lightning Source LLC
Chambersburg PA
CBHW070739160426
43192CB00009B/1494